Playhouses

A MEMOIR BY
Sherry Scott

Black Rose Writing | Texas

©2022 by Sherry Scott
All rights reserved. No part of this book may be reproduced, stored in a retrieval system or transmitted in any form or by any means without the prior written permission of the publishers, except by a reviewer who may quote brief passages in a review to be printed in a newspaper, magazine or journal.

The author grants the final approval for this literary material.

First printing

Some names and identifying details have been changed to protect the privacy of individuals.

ISBN: 978-1-68433-887-0
PUBLISHED BY BLACK ROSE WRITING
www.blackrosewriting.com

Printed in the United States of America
Suggested Retail Price (SRP) $15.95

Playhouses is printed in Sabon

*As a planet-friendly publisher, Black Rose Writing does its best to eliminate unnecessary waste to reduce paper usage and energy costs, while never compromising the reading experience. As a result, the final word count vs. page count may not meet common expectations.

Dedicated to my cousins
Diana and Iain (Karen) Shields,
and to those who broaden the way

Acknowledgments

I would like to thank my editor, Stephanie Lane, for journeying with me on another project. Your professionalism and commitment to conveying my vision onto the page always makes for a better ending. You make the way less lonely.

Thanks to David and Ginger Cook for their professional expertise and providing the visuals that fit the purpose. I treasure your pats on the back.

Special thanks to those I live with who may not always understand my obsession with making a mark but always support my efforts for trying. Thank you, Cliff Scott, for providing a space to create and for believing. Thank you, Aaron, Madison, Tyler, and Aubry, for embodying the reason why giving up is never an option when such wonder happens in its own time.

Thank you to the readers and encouragers: Bruce Noll, Dr. Peter Anderson, Jack Brannon, and to the beautiful Naomi Shihab Nye, who "always writes back."

I wish my parents, Vinson and Fay Shields, were still here so I could thank them for always providing a safe place.

Playhouses

"Be kind to yourself. Be kind to each other. Be kind to Mother Earth."
**Dr. James Allen Smith (1928–1993),
Austin College Baccalaureate, 1989**

Part 1

What I Knew

Chapter 1

Early memory: We were small, just the two of us out on the white-rock drive in front of our grandparents' farmhouse on a Sunday afternoon. I pushed the little red wagon and you pulled—you, with the strawberry blond head of board-straight, fly-away hair and I, with the unruly dark-haired mop. We were both without shoes, as usual, pants that didn't fit our legs-too-long-for-our-bodies, and shirts surely stained from Sunday dinner.

We had escaped the noon-day ritual after scooting mashed potatoes around our plates and were free under the North Texas blue sky until later called in for supper, baths, and other nonsense. The contents within our wagon were meaningful: rocks, bits of Tinkertoys, and sticks from underneath the black walnut tree. Their significance I can't recall, but it was a glorious game of shared towing between the two of us. The day changed when a directed movement caught your eye. "It's a snake!" Turning from my determined mission path, I saw a dark, straight object in the driveway, atop a mound of rock that our granddad had not smoothed out. "It's a stick," I replied, though not without some excitement in my voice.

We ventured slowly toward the rock pile, with me in the lead, to see if the stick would move. The stick stretched itself and wagged its tongue as the sun glinted off its coppery surface.

"Snake!" "Snake!" We turned and ran without looking behind to see if it was in snaking pursuit, until breathlessly we yanked open the left door off the front porch that yielded direct vision into the kitchen where they were all still sitting. (Didn't dinner ever end for these people?) I had beaten my cousin as usual, but as excited as we both were to tell first, our peals of "Snake! Snake!" crescendoed together in such alarm that we had them scrambling from the table.

There he sat, with his tongue darting back and forth, his head wagging menacingly. The adults immediately turned and interpreted: "That means stay away." Someone, namely Granddad, must have exited the back kitchen door toward the shed where he parked the pickup truck to get the hoe, for my next startled memory was the wagging head and darting tongue lying distinct and separate from the rest of the curved stick. "Stay away from that; it's just as dangerous dead as alive." Huh? But the head *was* still alive, darting and wagging in defiance—of course we weren't going near something that had tricked us so vilely. It had intruded into our sanctum of pretend from which we were sorely often torn.

Chapter 2

We were cousins separated by three months. (I was keenly aware my birthright in November clearly trumped her February arrival.) We were the first-born daughters of our fathers—two brothers named Shields, separated themselves by thirteen years. My only sibling was my brother, eleven and a half years older. Born on the same day as my paternal grandfather, my brother had basked in the undivided attention of my grandparents preceding my birth, a privilege that he profoundly missed once *we* came on the scene. Three years later, my cousin's sister was born, flipping the hierarchy on end and thrusting the initial three out of the limelight of our grandparents' favored attention. She was cute, chubby, grew to be more than the handful she hinted at as a baby, and was continually excluded by us.

My cousin, Diana Lynn, whose middle name was after her father, was affectionately called Dini—most likely first dubbed by my failed enunciation. She had missed the 1950s by two months; I had tenaciously hung on by a little less than two months. We were bound together before we could remember, though time and space came between us more than the days we shared. Our bond was secrecy and exclusion, primarily from my youngest cousin Karen, and apart from the scrutiny of the adults who seemed always to speculate the worst in us.

In reference to the preceding early memory, my grandmother (Granny hereafter) argued for years that we had left "that baby" in the wagon next to the snake in our rush to be the first to report the intruder. "Well, I know good and well that I went out there and grabbed her up from out of the wagon."

Not true! We would have *never* let her ride in such a hallowed space in the middle of our afternoon game. She was seated at the table in her highchair and was most likely left to stuff down more potatoes as the adults raced out the door.

Days spent at my grandparents' farm formed the foundation of our cohesiveness. No matter the time that had passed between us, the happenings in our lives—mundane or otherwise—were all dismissed as yesterday when our imaginary world picked up from where we had left off. The leaving off was very much out of our control, due to marriages and careers. My uncle Denny was in the United States Air Force, and, outside of deployments, was primarily stationed much farther south in Texas. The marriage was another issue that would someday loom over our coveted time together as a more daunting threat than his stint in Vietnam.

Our times spent together there are best recounted in seasons of the year, for we were young and protected for a short while from the passage of time that would occur within us. It was when the dawning of a day opened our sleeping eyelids with glad anticipation. I couldn't wait to get started even though I was intrigued by how long my cousin could sleep in. Because I attributed this to the more interesting places she lived (on a military base in San Antonio, Texas), I tried to imitate her. I would feign sleep for as long as I could, until finally I either roused her or gave up and made my way to the breakfast table. At least I got the pick of the bowl, an old, oblong piece of stoneware deemed for holding our buttered, sugar-laden oatmeal. Our day from then on, unless interrupted by structured plans from adults, consisted of a series of out and away excursions interrupted by in-and-out returns to the house, for however long it took to glean what we needed for sustenance and infrastructure to support the imaginary world we were creating.

Chapter 3

Summer on a rural ninety-acre piece of land in Texas was the closest thing to paradise I could imagine, because it was "the perfect day" sung from the old hymnal: nothing lacking. If perhaps there was lack, we were so happy in our blissful ignorance we didn't miss it—much like the interpretation of heaven my granny used to give. When asked if we would know each other in heaven, she emphatically replied, "No." Her Baptist understanding was that if her *boys* weren't saved, how could it be heaven if she knew they weren't there? I argued vehemently, what good was heaven if we didn't know each other?—too young to boil it down to "Then what's the point?" But a summer day spent on the farm was a paradigm that artists sometimes capture deep within canvases of golden light descending over the land.

The simple pleasures of lark song and growing things, enough to awaken all our senses, centered around a plain white, two-story farmhouse that remained glued together by tenacity and a little aid from running water, rural electric, spit and nails. It sheltered us and fed us—body and soul. It opened itself onto a front porch that beheld the earth's finest gardening hour and proceeded around back to the singsong of the slapping screen door, wafting scents of butter and vanilla through its tiny pores. Its nooks and crannies were devoid of precious material things but held hours of self-evolved fun on the foundation of its linoleum floors and under the eaves of its pitched roof. Our laughter spilled out its thick windows adorned with cheap plastic stippled curtains, pulled to the side to let the hot air pass in and out.

The huge, Zenith floor-model deep freeze that held Granny's hard-earned achievements of plucked chickens, frozen peaches, and beans served as our long dining room table in the middle of a great hall. Royalty sat at one end while Karen was exiled far to the other. Granddad's swivel easy chair, stocky and grotesquely re-covered in maroon vinyl served as a merry-go-round for extended periods until, bored with the game, we flung our younger cousin onto the floor after tempting her to topple us from the throne. And to the overheard tune of the party line where she prattled with the local Baptist women over someone's hospitalization gone south, we delighted in the home-baked goodness of Granny's cooking, until the swaying song of greening grasses called us outside to play.

What centered our paradise—contained within the off-limits farm-to-market road that ran in front and the country cemetery just back of Granddad's pasture—was the house and a series of buildings and plots of sweet significance and memory. An acre's worth of garden stood proudly in front of the house, bordered with as many flowers as the tomato vines and rows of beans Granny tended daily. The cellar in the side yard held Granny's canning, primarily beets and pickles that positively glowed in the dark due to excessive food coloring. Off to the side stood the brooder house, used mainly in the early spring. The larger hen house stood next, up against the pasture fence that enclosed a horse who drank from the primitive washing machine tank placed strategically close to the water spigot with an attached yellow rubber hose. Behind the house stood an aging structure deemed the smokehouse, devoid of its original function and paint. It was a raw, scary place to explore, particularly without shoes. Its rotting wooden floors were scattered with nails and hardware scraps overshadowed by faded cabinets. It resembled a deserted kitchen with broken pieces except for the numerous wild cats that scrambled when we tentatively entered its open doorway. The cats became a distant memory until, years later, my dad revealed that Granny had asked my uncle to rid the place of them. With his drawn pistol out the back door, my uncle targeted any moving part of a cat. Dad said the yellow fur was flying.

Adjacent to the dismembered smokehouse, which was eventually torn down, stood a happier place—a small open shed, primarily used for storage. Its corrugated tin roof offered the only protection to its contents. The back and sides of the three-walled structure refused to meet the roof, thus offering a great view of the back pastures that lay just on the other side. It became one of our designated summer playhouses, because the air moved freer. Granddad's pickup shed stood next to a painted rail fence on the side of the house within the shade of the great black walnut tree. Beyond the fence gate, the side pasture held an array of farm equipment and metal scraps under a huge bottom-land post oak tree before reaching the once painted barn with its grain cellar, animal pens, and hayloft. A spring-fed creek ran the length of the farm between the pastures and corn field. It was as picturesque as the Shenandoah Valley to an unkempt band of cousins who explored its every corner.

Summer was fraught with its intrusions, but the wildness about the place we loved supported these intrusions as well. On more than one occasion, a snake suddenly heralded its presence, much to our dismay. The stuff that feeds nightmares, that ventures its way through the subconscious during sleep, I first encountered on the farm. The image of a nine-foot, silvery, spineless object traversing through the grass where I regularly stepped barefooted, resurfaced for decades. When amidst the frolicking itchy fun in the hayloft we spotted a coppery, coiled structure watching us from the corner, the cutout hole in the middle of the loft we'd avoided for fear of falling became a point of quick escape rather than a yawning abyss. And then there were the yellow jacket nests, the dirt dauber nests, hot peppers on the vines, rusted nails, and chigger bites that marched around our waist bands in the summer heat that fretted our sleep. There was nothing left to do but scratch, toss, and turn in the thick night air. Yet another intruder was a welcomed distraction, though we would never have admitted it at the time, for she was the subject of delicious handed-down tales.

Estelle was Granny's visiting friend who lived atop the crest of a white-rock road that traveled parallel to our grandparents' farm on the other side of the hen house. She and her sister were two old maids bearing the name Baxter under the same small roof. She looked every bit the movie version of a southern spinster. Her hair was wavy and pinned at the nape of her neck; her front teeth were unabashedly filled with gold here and there, and her dark print jersey dresses swished below her thin knees and above the black lace-up shoes she always wore. But the face and the voice were what we lived for as well as ran from. We could count on her nose being thickly powdered, her cheeks rouged fuchsia, and red lipstick smeared in the corners of her mouth and atop her front teeth. The purse held on her forearm like so, a white embroidered hankie in hand, and coos of "Aaaww, the sweet little things" were other certainties. It was as though she had never seen children, the way she thrilled over pulling us to her, covering our dirty faces with red lipstick, and continually repeating the above phrase all the times we saw her.

Her dark 1940s model sedan plowing up white dust in the front drive signaled her arrival, and we dove under the cool shade of the house every time. But eventually our curiosity over betting she would repeat the same ritual overpowered our need to stay hidden, and we would venture forth to hear that voice squeezed out between her off-centered teeth. We squirmed and giggled while enduring the barrage of her kisses. We lived for an afternoon of iconic Estelle. It would have broken our hearts to have witnessed her decline, which occurred before our grandparents' deaths. Other changes would also signal an end to our blissful summers.

Chapter 4

Recollections of winters on the farm centered on the two celebrated events of Christmas and its distant cousin—Thanksgiving. My cousins were rarely there for Thanksgiving, so, disappointment over their absence was coupled with the dismay of learning Granny usually served roast chicken with her dressing and trimmings instead of the celebrated bigger bird. The first grade had opened up a world of expressive language, so I had become increasingly aware of Butterball's advertising campaign of the turkey as an American centerpiece. "It just has to be turkey in order to qualify as Thanksgiving!" Christmas however, fondly established itself in the halls of memory, because it was based on more than just a meal, something my cousin and I disdained. Baked sweets and presents promised at the end of dinner kept us diligently picking through everything else drowned in gravy.

Christmas meant a week-long visit from my cousin's family. It was a concentrated celebration due to my uncle's military leave to come home, so we wasted no time in sizing up one another to see if I was still a little taller than Dini since I was still two months older. It was a time of re-bonding and re-exploration: how much had changed since we had been there last? Did the farm still bear traces of what we had left behind, things we had discovered and hidden again for safe keeping, places we had marked as our own? It meant re-establishing our territory, a jealous tug of war between us and Karen—to include her or not include her.

Our jealousy was driven by her favoritism, clearly exposed in the distribution of gifts, and most outlandishly demonstrated by our grandparents. There was never any doubt the kid was cute and had personality to boot. The orneriness of Karen was so pervasive that, a generation removed, when my first-born child exhibited self-proclaiming behavior, my mother jokingly nicknamed him "Karen Elizabeth." Blond, blue-eyed, dimples everywhere (sustained by her sometimes-habit of eating butter sticks right out of the refrigerator), the youngest and last—she was a shoo-in for best-in-show. "But it doesn't have to be quite so obvious!" complained the two runners-up who schemed to make her pay for such audacity.

We tore open the corners of her Christmas gifts to reveal the conspiracy against us. The three-foot-tall package deemed Karen's contained a life-size doll, and our flat packages were surely matching shirt and pant sets, again! (Not that Karen or Dini ever wanted a doll; but I surely did.) We got in trouble for that one as well as the time we *doctored* her iced tea.

While sitting at our designated place for dinner one day, we decided to have a little innocent fun while Karen was in the bathroom. Our plates contained the usual concoction of thoroughly mashed potatoes, fried meat the grown-ups had cut in pieces, vegetables, and biscuits. We began layering her tea with bits from our plates: a dab of potatoes floating over the ice, then some chicken fried steak, a little green bean, topped off with a crumbled biscuit to hold the gravy. It was glorious. From out of nowhere, she started this insane bawling when she returned to find our meal-in-a-glass sculpture. She duped the adults into thinking it was a plot against her, and we got in trouble over behaving so terribly.

Family conversations centered around Karen: regarding the day's mishaps, her temperament, her cute mispronunciations, and her myriad of unfounded fears—so we thought. The absolute worst was the betrayal of our granddad, who on occasion snuck off in the pickup for a store-run with Karen alone in the front seat beside him. M&M's were the "stuff of our lives," and we couldn't be sure that she hadn't gotten more than we had. Oh, there would be hell to pay, and what better way to reap our due than assigning our usual roles of play.

Chapter 5

An integral part of our play on the property were playhouses, or rather structures on the farm appropriated for our playhouses (i.e., tool shed, chicken brooding house, cellar). They drew us together every time we congregated as families, like migrating geese returning to the same wildlife refuge annually. The changing location reflected the time of year, offering more shelter, less of a view, and vice versa. The brooder house was ideal for wintertime play because of its walls, roof, and its windows that could be shuttered. The floor was dirt, of course, to accommodate the fifty or so baby chicks that would be coming via mail carrier in the spring. The best feature was that it contained two rooms: one designated as kitchen and living area, the other as the bedroom—big enough to hold one of our old baby beds that Dini ultimately managed to collapse by running and jumping into its middle. KABAM!

So, first order of the day upon returning to the farm was to assess the damage done by time and our grandparents. Had they set aside our junk to move in their own junk: wheelbarrow, tools, canning jars? Was the structure still sound; did we need to make some obvious repairs? At the very least we needed to commandeer Granny's broom to sweep the dirt and cobwebs aside. After adding to the place's aesthetic appeal with whatever we could find to embellish the surroundings, we set about that most momentous task of assigning roles.

We played house within the familiar constraints of what was portrayed in *Family Circle Magazine,* circa 1964: husband-breadwinner, wife-homemaker, and bothersome children to support. We went into our routine like a scripted play. Dini was the father, and I was the mother; then there was Karen. The older she got, the bigger the fuss she made over wanting to be the dad as well. It went something like this:

"I want to be the dad!"

"No. Dini is the dad. She is always the dad."

"But I want to be the dad!"

"No! You have to be the kid. You can be Mike."

"No! I don't want to be the kid. I want to be the dad!"

"You have to be Mike!"

"NO! I don't want to be Mike!"

"Then you can't play."

After we established the roles (with however much force it took to sway the game to our advantage), we resumed "playing house" from where we had left off last time. The winter playhouse was thrilling in that we were battling the elements—our imaginations had to soar despite our confinement. The chores of the family and particularly that of the provider (who had to care for the cows and land, along with Mike, who helped feed livestock and gather the firewood) were dutifully supported by me, back home tending the fire and cooking. Oh, we had it down. By the end of the day, even Karen had settled into her role, as our trio blended into the family that sustained itself against the wintry blast with only an occasional slip into the farmhouse for stolen provisions.

The summer playhouse was eventually groomed into the paradise above all previous attempts at housekeeping, as our old Christmas presents began taking up residence instead of Granddad's farm implements. Because my cousins had to pack lightly from each residence to another assignment mandated by the U.S. Air Force, their metal kitchen play stove and accessories were transplanted to the farm. With my family's own move, the table and chairs and kitchen cupboard my dad made me landed there as well. With an open view of Granddad's wheat fields behind us, our table was even festooned with a vase of Granny's flowers while simple cotton material billowed out the sides as makeshift curtains. Sadly, it was to be the grand finale of playhouses on the farm. It was the last place we would gather before our grandparents sold the property and moved into "town": Tom Bean, Texas, population 500.

I'm sure remnants of our play were unearthed for years after our grandparents left the place. Our tin plates, bits of cups and saucers, plastic bits of arms and toes of dolls and toy soldiers were most likely tilled up and stumbled upon until the earth or the trash finally claimed them all. I personally found vestiges of play my cousins left under a lone pear tree along the fence edging the garden. My cousins had played there while Granny worked the garden. Left behind were bits of toys, rocks, and a plastic bumblebee, symbolic of the real flying species that must have buzzed around their heads within the perfume of the budding tree. It was a bittersweet find. It foretold profound changes in our relationship that, all too soon, time would reveal. Even though my grandparents' impending move was still a secret at the time of my discovery, I somehow sensed that the cousins would never return to that place. Whenever their travels brought them back to us, our play would certainly resume with our respected roles intact: Dini, the father; I, the mother; and Karen, portraying our contentious son. *This* would not change. To expect any sort of straying from this premise would be to deny who we were.

Chapter 6

Though our playtime was interrupted by the loss of "our farm," Vietnam, and a messy divorce, we picked up where we left off the next time either the holidays or summer break deemed it time for a visit. A new playhouse never materialized as such on my grandparents' new property, but we still played house. There was the acre-sized garden in the middle of town, the storm cellar in the middle of the garden, Granny's kitchen smells, and Granddad's old pickup that still traveled between the store and cow pasture—all tangibles of our times together. For a little while, our sense of playtime remained the same with a notable exception: we now had town roads on which to ride bikes.

Small-town dirt roads traveled on an old, shared bike of Dini's (unless Dad loaded mine in his truck) became busy highways and city streets of commerce. There was so much to do: take the kids to school, pick up someone from the airport, drive back and forth from work, run errands, buy groceries, pay the water bill, and retrieve kids from school. We had become independently mobile, apart from rides in the bed of the pickup. But our rides through town always brought us back to the small white framed house on the corner of two streets we never thought enough of to learn the names. Years later, my granny confided in me that her best years with her grandchildren had occurred on the farm.

Prior to my grandparents' move, my own family had moved closer to them. We were twenty minutes down the road, in Sherman, population 36,000, larger than my previous place of residence by 10,000 people. Now that I was closer, my cousins, when in town, could spend the night at my house as well as with their grandmothers, who now lived across from each other on the same corner. This time around, our making it through a sleepover together hinged more on Karen's nighttime anxieties. After my dad had to get out of bed one night and drive the crying child back to where her mother was staying (even after Dini had threatened her within an inch of her life to "shut up"), adventures between *just the two of us* continued beautifully.

Our games of playing house evolved into laboratories of experiments afforded by the bathroom. Our favorite game was concocting potions and designing patterns on the medium of toilet paper. Utilizing my mom's half bath and our family's full bathroom, we individually carried out experiments within our designated labs. We rolled out long sheets of toilet paper from their respected holders, squirted ribbons of lotion on the inner surface, and then folded the paper in stackable waves. We let this art form sit on the top of the closed toilet lid while we busied ourselves brewing the next medical breakthrough from various substances found in the medicine cabinet. After a time, we unfolded the toilet paper to compare designs left by the lotion squished between the layers. For some strange reason (becoming increasingly stranger to me now), this ritual was as important as the mixture that was evolving from foot powder, ear drops, isopropyl alcohol, facial cleanser, cough syrup, and other unidentified entities with labels we couldn't read. The experiments concluded with a mandatory test run: we had to taste the mixture. A single swallow was all we ever managed.

Stranger still, our bathroom laboratory experiments were not the reason we were expelled from the bathroom. (Mom and Dad never caught on to that.) It was the designated bathtime. This was the first house between the three of us that came with a showerhead. The combination of filling the bathtub to a dangerous level with the showerhead on—while ignoring Karen's whiny cries—made for some fantastic water fun. The best attempt at a full-on water slide experience was when we soaped down the tub and used the back incline to launch ourselves into the rapidly filling bath. (To think that my dad's biggest concern was over someone using up all the hot water.) After water began spilling out into the hallway from underneath the bathroom door, we were heralded out and subsequently not allowed to bathe together, ever.

Because our times together became increasingly fewer, our playtime often turned to bringing each other up to date. Dini and Karen's parents had finally split for good after a series of separations. Just before my uncle's stint in Vietnam, my aunt had taken up bartending to help support the family. I thought this arrangement strange when my family and I visited them during their posted time at San Antonio's Lackland Air Force Base. My aunt left for her nighttime shift while the rest of us conversed, watched television, bathed, and went to bed. Apparently, an affair had developed and continued off and on during my uncle's tour. It was back and forth—sandwiched with pleas for mercy and permission to come back home—until my uncle issued an ultimatum: no more returns if she chose to leave again. After leaving Texas, my cousins were relegated to life spent with their mother and her lover, in and out of motel rooms between California and Tucson, Arizona.

At the ripe age of ten years old, we were sitting on my new French provincial canopied bed when my cousin began to divulge secrets of the past year in her unique but hilarious way. Just tripping off her tongue came this descriptive scene like something out of *Divorce Court:* While staying in an adjoining motel room, she had been suddenly awakened in the middle of the night by noises from her mother's room. Peeking through the door left ajar, she saw her mother, lying spread eagle on the bed, with her lover between her legs. She was repeatedly exclaiming, "Take it easy, take it easy!" After he removed himself, Dini watched her mother, still lying on her back in a frog-legged position, take a Kleenex from the side of the bed and wipe away a white substance from her nude self. Riding atop my new plastic blow-up pillow printed with ladybugs, she laughingly exclaimed, "It was like watching a dog humping like crazy on another dog!" We released our collective giggles and forever let burst the bubble of child's play that had been performed from our bedrock of imagination. Our version of playhouses inhabited by family was forever changed.

"What about Karen?" I asked.

"Oh, she was asleep," she said.

Chapter 7

A series of broken coming-togethers and partings became the new and difficult norm. Karen lived intermittently with my grandparents while my uncle was overseas; Dini was shifted for short stints between her mom and relatives.

One of our saddest moments came while waiting for the Sunday evening service of the Tom Bean First Baptist Church to let out. I stood in the side yard of my grandparents' house, looking up the road expectantly at the church's orange painted front doors and the parking lot to the west side of the building. My parents had brought me to spend the night, and I was delirious with the promise of getting to see Dini, who had gone to church with her other grandmother. (Karen was living with my grandparents at the time.) Such was not to be the case. My aunt's brother, Johnny, was also waiting outside the church to escort Dini into a car and off to his family's home in the Dallas area. My cousin's stay with her uncle, aunt, and their two boys lasted a couple of months. They decorated her room in pink and insisted she conform to their conservative view on how a young lady should dress. She had been enrolled in school but was subsequently jerked out and returned to her mother, who left Texas for Arizona with both sisters in tow. I saw Dini only once during that time.

One constant was Karen's anxiety and disruptive behavior. She had always been difficult due to our grandparents' spoiling, but her current outbursts were something for which they were unprepared, no matter Karen's position as favorite. She was the only grandchild my granny ever spanked, though she had come close to wringing my brother's neck one cold day, when he threw her head scarf she'd made him wear into the pig's pen. My granny simply did not know what to do with this disturbed, stubborn child who clung to both grandparents with a sense of urgency. Karen, a school-aged child, could not or would not go to the bathroom by herself in their tiny framed house—a subject that was casually discussed around the Christmas tree one year.

"She'll say, 'Come on, Granny, we have to go,' and I have to go with her," Granny matter-of-factly told.

My granddad, who dearly loved Karen, took a quieter approach with her but could be provoked if pushed too far. During one confrontation, she got in his face and repeatedly yelled, "Liar! Liar!" He used the belt in that incident, which he later sorely regretted. I witnessed an interchange between them that was more likely routine rather than exception. He was enjoying the baseball game from his easy chair one evening when Karen came strutting in from outside, swung his elderly skinny legs aside like they were twigs and marched on toward the refrigerator.

"I'll knock the fire out of you," he irritably muttered under his breath, regaining his seated posture. My dad doubled over in laughter.

The dictates in the house had changed. It was clear to my parents: my grandparents were not equipped to handle the situation. Even clearer to me, years later, was the missed fact that Karen had been abused.

Urinary tract problems had long affected both cousins. Accidents were common, and stories of the many times I caused Dini to wet her pants by either making her laugh uncontrollably or impeding her from getting to the bathroom on time were legend. However, Karen's accidents were punctuated by recurring nightmares, fears, and anxieties that fueled raging, tearful outbursts. Whether Karen was abused by neglect, emotionally, physically, sexually, or a combination of any, Dini verified one certainty: Karen was not tolerated by the man my aunt lived with and eventually married. He said Karen got in the way; she was too loud, too disturbed. Karen therefore clung to the only constant in her life, Dini, especially after being torn from my grandparents for good.

Interruptions and moves continued throughout their formative years, until a period of relative stability occurred in their adolescence, for Dini, anyway. After a prolonged time away in Arizona, the two moved back with their dad, who by that time had remarried and was father to a beautiful stepdaughter, Glenda. Glenda and Diana (called by her formal name thereon) formed an immediate attachment, which left Karen, once again, out in the cold. Navigating the difficult years of awkwardness, punctuated by peer and family pressures, would only serve to charge the atmosphere in the newly blended home. Sadly, this period proved to be the tipping point for Karen and Diana. Years later, my youngest cousin would tell her sister, "I will never forgive you."

I can't help thinking that Karen's declaration was related to Diana's not being able to protect her—more than it related to her exile. After all, we had been leaving out Karen for years. Upon one of her returns to Texas after a short stint living with her mom Diana promptly shared with me her own story. One sunny Saturday afternoon, she was violated by her stepfather while watching television on the couch. Her mother was at the grocery store. We were driving around in my 1970s orange VW Bug, while she relayed the event. In my naivete, I questioned her about her resistance.

"Yeah, I fought him off, with everything I had in me!"

It was unbelievable, like something out of a tabloid, like something that could have been avoided. We never discussed it again.

Chapter 8

Games involving intimacy with my cousins and certain playmates were as innocent as my discovering a thick, white, sweet-smelling substance between my labia during preschool years. For a couple of nights in a row, I couldn't wait to get into bed under the covers, pull down my cotton underpants, and touch a small area between my legs that induced a strange excitatory sensation. I thought no more or less of that exploration than a weekly afterschool ritual of playing *doctor* with a friend in the second grade. Behind the locked door of her family bathroom, which contained a long white marble countertop (an amenity my house never had), we took turns pretending to take each other's rectal temperature with the rounded end of a bobby pin. Emulating the exam with a sense of naughtiness made the act pleasantly stimulating compared to the dreadful experience many of us routinely encountered at doctors' offices in the 1960s.

When my cousins and I played house, intimacy consisted of stealing kisses or holding hands. We mirrored the lives of the adults around us while setting up our own household. As we got older, time not only separated us but hid certain physical changes that popped up unexpectedly upon our sporadic reunions. I was roughly three months older than Diana, but she was years ahead in physical development.

The beginning interplay between the hypothalamus gland to the pituitary gland to the targeted sex organs of her body had been set in motion during an extended time away from our grandparents, hence her appearance took me aback one cold Christmas vacation. After a prolonged absence, Diana and Karen were deposited for a brief stay in Tom Bean. I had only seen Sacramento in a mailed Polaroid photo, showing the two sisters playing in some snow along the roadside. It was as unfamiliar to me as the way Diana looked upon her return. Her new breasts made her button-down plaid shirt stand straight out in front of her body. Karen gleefully remarked, "They're like Coke bottles!" particularly when compared to my adolescent body, which looked as if it were stuck in elementary school. Karen remained pre-adolescent, except that her burgeoning weight afforded the need for a training bra. But, as usual, after an awkward period of sizing up one another, we started from where we had left off.

Just before my cousins left for the longest exodus of our early adolescent years, we played a game under the protection of nightfall and lights-out in Granny's bedroom. There was a cot next to Granny's side of the bed for Karen to sleep on when she came to visit; it was carried over from her sporadic stays there. We pretended it was a bed in a brothel, on which we took turns being the one who was purchased and the purchaser. Though there was no interchange of money, real or imagined, the concept was the same: there was a designated period of exploration by one upon the other.

Diana was much more adept at fondling than I. Kissing was easy between us—we emulated the Elvis Presley movies we had seen growing up. However, when it came to removing our shirts and massaging the other's body as a perceived ritual one does in a place imagined like that, I was okay with receiving but not reciprocating. For one thing, my pre-adolescent chest had not the slightest sign of development nor the capacity for stimulation. Diana's body, conversely, had become an unknown and scary place. Her breasts were foreign, and I couldn't bring myself to massage them vigorously while we were kissing, the way she had done. I kind of skirted around the outside perimeter, carefully avoiding her enlarged nipples. The game may have proven frustrating for her, but, as in all our games together, we eventually got bored and moved onto something else. We were just as likely to have abandoned the game due to Karen's persistent whining and knock at the door regarding her lack of turns and threatening to tell on us if she were not allowed in.

But another example of intimacy shared between us had nothing to do with touch and remains a vivid memory. During another Christmas holiday when we were about ten or eleven, we ventured around town on bikes and stopped at Tom Bean's only café to warm ourselves. The little framed structure on a pier and beam foundation occupied the northwest corner on Main Street, shy of the yellow flashing light over the farm-to-market road that ran through town. It was littered with metal four-top tables and chairs, a pick-up counter with a bell, and a cash register on the way out. Open Monday through Friday, it was heavily frequented during the lunch hour by farmers and field hands who wanted a home-style cooked dinner. (Rural areas in the South used to refer to the noonday meal as dinner, because it was usually a hot cooked meal with all the trimmings, saving lighter fare for *supper* in the evening.) The lunch hour had passed, so we sat at an isolated table and ordered hot cocoa.

As a child, I was not one for hot drinks, even hot cocoa, but Diana enjoyed them and even drank coffee at her grandmother's house—something I never understood. Hard as I tried, dumping mounds of sugar and dousing the hot liquid with milk, I could not muster her adult habit of drinking a cup of coffee. So, there we were, seated in an emptying café with thick mugs of steaming cocoa, going through our "imitation of life" scenario: husband meets wife for coffee. Like something from a scene in *As The World Turns* (watched religiously by our grandparents after the midday meal), we began our conversation by mimicking the '60s characters of bitchy Lisa and her do-gooder husband, Dr. Bob Hughes. (Not that we played the characters, but we imitated their marital tensions leading to that dreaded dark word, D-I-V-O-R-C-E.)

Diana played her part so well. She sat across the table, her hands conformed around the coffee cup as naturally as the adults in my family, intermittently sipping the hot concoction, staring intently into my eyes. It was an unnerving moment. It wasn't as if I interpreted her gestures as anything threatening or unnamed, but I felt a little flushed. I was suddenly shy in front of the cousin I had known since having our pictures taken together in our first year of life. It was only a pretend conversation between a man and woman, but it was so easily accessed because of the familiarity with our roles. She was who she was; I was who I was. It had always been that way. It was what I always knew, what I always counted on, and to reverse the roles would have been unimaginable.

Part 2

What I Was Told

Chapter 9

Time and distance proved not to be the only separating factors between the cousins' lives and mine. During their prolonged absence I had discovered religion while Diana pursued the ROTC and basketball.

Though we all traveled in and out the Southern Baptist doors of my grandparents' church at various times, I had been raised in the Presbyterian church by my parents, who both rejected limitations of Baptist teaching. My cousins were Air Force brats and children of divorce whose primary ideas about faith originated from my grandparents but knew many detours. Soon after my twelfth birthday, ironically in February (Diana's birth month), I began attending a Pentecostal church on Sunday evenings with a close neighborhood friend. This would prove to be no little casually passing phase.

Drawn to the charismatic, boisterous worship style that was rooted in the holy-roller deep Southeast, I slowly began to withdraw from the structured religious gatherings that had nurtured me since I was a young child. By the eighth grade, I was attending Sunday morning and Sunday evening services apart from my parents and participating in all the youth and choir events I was allowed. By early high school I was participating eagerly in the Sunday morning bus ministry that required knocking doors on Saturday mornings and accompanying kids on the bus to and from Sunday school. By age sixteen, I added regular Wednesday night services to my weekly scheduled attendances at the church, including youth group choir practice on Friday nights and Saturday nights at the youth building. As my inclusion within the church grew, the separation within my own family widened.

Kudos to understanding parents who afforded me spiritual curiosity, possibly rooted in their own partings from traditions of the Baptist and Church of Christ houses of faith. But what they nor I readily recognized was the longstanding consequence of entering such an exclusively held view: "looking on from the outside does not convey the truth of being on the inside." In other words, *the straight and narrow way* was designed for the few and enlightened, and the separation from others in the form of dress, lifestyle, and obsessive worship sealed the belief that the more misunderstood *we* were, the more living proof that the church's *persecution in the end times* belonged exclusively to *us*. One had to suffer non-conformity in an open, if not old-fashioned way, to live out one's faith. The rejection of other mainstream religions and their practices and vice versa, served to comfort believers that we were the *only* rightful travelers along the path that led to eternal life.

These were years of long separations from my cousins. Little did I know they were carving out lives for themselves, rooted in *How to survive a broken family while Mom indulges herself*. The changes occurring rapidly within my own newly discovered way of life were so fascinating and consuming that I gave little thought to the pair whose parting had stung as bad as losing a best friend that "sticketh closer than a brother."

Chapter 10

February 1972: *Aliknodihea, ejoihobldhdos, ghisboldishcoooooosa, speceekahosiaskda, mehaliollopidquis.* The baptism of the Holy Ghost fell on me at twelve years of age in front of a Pentecostal altar. While on my knees, an aura of light and peace surrounded me as I faintly heard myself saying a flow of words that I did not understand. Speaking in tongues as the Holy Ghost gave utterance was unexplainable, indescribable, and unwritable.

This was not the first altar call I had answered. I was prone to answering the guilt-tripped persistent sway of the Baptist invitational while attending worship services or vacation bible school with friends; there was no such thing in our Presbyterian church. I had witnessed many a tearful soul *down front* at my grandparents' Baptist church. When I was very young, I once asked Granny why they were crying so; her reply seemed to indicate I should already know why or it was something about which she didn't care to elaborate: "Oh, it's an emotional thing." But as pressuring as these calls felt to a young person trying to be good and assure herself a place with God in the future (if all these horrible things were truly about to happen), they usually involved nothing more than signing a card with my shaking hand while wiping tears of fear and repentance with the other. Repeating an allegiance to

Jesus as my Savior was no big revelation; I had been singing *Jesus Loves Me* since the age of three. But the altar call in a Pentecostal church was a separate ritual; it was a service in and of itself and could last hours.

The first time I answered the call to come down to receive the Holy Ghost was a spontaneous response to the aforementioned pull. Sunday night was labeled the Evangelical Service and lasted longer than the standard Pentecostal Sunday morning hour. It began with a rousing song service, which included refrain after refrain of known choruses by the church, followed by prayer anointing of the sick, a word or two from the preacher, an offering, a packed youth choir rocking two selections that had the whole front-row alto section in tears, and unless the spirit spurred a *run-away service*, a roughly one-hour sermon that led directly into the altar call. It was always initiated by the pastor's wife moving quietly toward the piano. She began an emotionally moving, or sometimes even mournful chorus, accompanied by the congregation in hushed tones, that continued during the pastor's repeated invitations to experience tangible salvation.

The two long solid wood altars were pillars of ritual in the front of the sanctuary, located beneath and on either side of the pulpit. As people gathered there either in need of "praying through" (a phrase that essentially meant repenting of sin that had caused one's faith to regress and praying through to a state of joyful renewal) or filling of the Holy Ghost, the organ and piano music kept playing while the lights in the church were dimmed except the overhead spotlight, which gave the altar time a feeling of intimacy or increased urgency, depending on how you looked at it. "Prayer warriors" (people of the congregation who felt a calling to pray effectively and loudly with those who responded) surrounded those at the altar as others simply came forth to pray on their own, covering the floor and the carpeted steps leading up to the chancel (though I never heard it called the chancel in the Pentecostal church) and sometimes kneeling before the first-row pews or in the aisles. The more wayward the person, a first-time responder or someone returning to the flock after a long hiatus, the bigger the draw for an enthusiastic prayer-support crowd.

Because I was a twelve-year-old child of no significance, I did not attract much attention the first time I visited that altar. I was surrounded and prayed over by my friends Donna and Shelley (who had brought me as a visitor with the promise of checking out their youth center afterward), their father, and two other school friends. The pastor administered a brief "laying on of hands" as he prayed for me before moving onto others. My first try was not a success. After a prolonged vigil of tears and lifting my hands in open prayer seeking God's indwelling presence, I sat on the carpeted floor spent and dejected. I had not received what I had gone to the altar for—the gift of the Holy Ghost evidenced by speaking in tongues. Under the glow of the spotlight above me in the stage-darkened church while the music played on, my friends' father soothed my fear of rejection. He told me the church altar was not the only place a person could pray and receive the Holy Ghost; a person could pray anywhere and open themselves up to God, even in the privacy of their own room.

This was particularly comforting for two reasons. First, I went down with two other friends, and one of them got it. It seemed so easy for her—why wasn't it for me? Second, I didn't know when I would be returning, because I was just a visitor. The hour was late, and my parents were waiting back home for my return. (We didn't go to the youth center after all. It was closed on Sundays.)

That night and for the rest of the week, I sat up in bed after lights out with my hands held up as I had seen practiced in the church and prayed for the Holy Ghost. Throughout the week, my inability to experience God's "other tongues," remained on my mind, though I did not share it with anyone, particularly my parents. I was lost. It was up to me to do something about it. I began to calculate the cost of separating from my church of origin and adopting a completely different mindset apart from my family's.

I could give up wearing pants (a long-standing *holiness* rule within the at-large Pentecostal church)—they didn't fit me properly anyway. I was too tall and thin; pants either fit in the waist and were therefore too short in length or the other way around. I could give up cutting my hair for good. I had recently obtained a pixie cut (just before the shag cut came out), and I was determined to let it grow unimpeded by scissors. I looked better with long hair anyway. I could give up going to the movies and football games since I wasn't old enough to sit in the student section at the local high school games. I could give up hanging out with a lot of my friends. I was never going to make the popular group if I hadn't made it by now; I could find a new set of friends.

My calculations never included giving up my family. I did not intend for my choice of worship to separate me from my immediate or extended family.

Unbeknownst to my parents, two weeks later, when I asked if I could attend Sunday night worship with my neighborhood friends, I had my young head set on obtaining something that came with a cost I was too naïve to understand. I was ready to sacrifice all that I had known as normal and commit to a life I was only beginning to explore. Everything must have been aligned as I knelt with a Sunday school teacher beside me. I experienced something I could not fake or explain away. It was a real happening within the context of complete childhood innocence. I felt changed. I felt liberated and was hungry for more. From that moment, I was prepared to do whatever it took to continue on the path I had willfully initiated.

Chapter 11

Life went on as usual for a sixth-grader other than scrounging around for a dress or skirt that came close to my knees instead of wearing a trusted pair of jeans. I went to school, played with my neighborhood friends, ate dinner at home, went to church with my parents Sunday mornings, went to Sunday night services with my best friends Shelley and Donna and their dad. My parents' only initial concern was the late hour I was dropped off after church—on a school night. They had difficulty understanding why services ran as long as three hours. While dependent on others for a ride home, I wasn't in a position to drag somebody away if the *spirit was moving*. The altar service was so uniquely loud and different that I preferred my parents did not come for me, out of fear they would not approve or understand.

The summer before starting the seventh grade was hallmarked by leaving some familiarities behind and embracing new ones. I was giving up ballet and piano classes that I had participated in since the second and third grade, respectively, for joining the youth choir. My junior high status made me eligible for being a part of the youth group. I was giving up all worldly associations to follow my newfound passion for God and the church's instruction. Singing in the choir required following the dress code. Dresses or skirts had to be to the knee and the hair had to be "worn up." The alarm that registered on the face of my mom the first time she saw a hairpiece atop my head after arriving home from service one night eclipsed her concern about the lateness of the hour.

Cosmetology classes at the local high school still taught hairpiece styling—a synthetic swath of hair that rested on a foam dummy after it was washed, curled, and styled like human hair. I had worn a *cascade* hairpiece in one of my ballet recitals: a bunch of curls that attached to the back of my head, with my real hair pinned up underneath, so the curls cascaded down my neck. I got the thing out and tried fixing it, but it had set in a drawer too long, and the curls were messy. My friend Donna took it to one of her high school friends who styled hairpieces for some of the church's women. My cascade came back poofed high atop the dummy head with curls from top to bottom. Donna secured my real hair under the thing and attached it to my head with what seemed like a hundred bobby pins. I looked positively Pentecostal after slipping into one of the two church dresses I wore over and over, on account of their both being dressier and longer. I came home that warm summer evening, elated after singing in the choir for the first time and enjoying pizza out with the high school kids. Mother was in for a surprise when she opened the door, for I had gotten dressed at my friends' home (which became the routine, so we could fix each other's hair). But I was happy, so Mom expressed her "Oh, my" and waved at my ride before closing the front door. I was already floating off to my room.

The only glitch of the night had been a compliment paid by one of the senior high Sunday school teachers who was a respected and well-liked businessman in the community. At the end of the service he stopped Shelley and me, both incoming seventh graders, to congratulate us on our choir debut. "I hope both of you take seriously your new responsibilities as members of the youth group and choir. You are taking a mature step toward representing the church, and people are counting on you." As we walked away the man overheard me as I turned and anxiously whispered to my friend, "Did he think my dress was too short?"

The next Sunday night, the preacher used my overheard worry as a humorous, tongue-in-cheek teaching moment, chuckling at my guilt-associated misinterpretation of a compliment. Though no names were mentioned, the pastor's daughter, with whom I would later become best friends, turned from the front row and gave me a knowing smile as laughter erupted. Only then as my cheeks burned did I realize that in my innocence I had misinterpreted the man's words. But I had always been a truth seeker, and, at age twelve, my ignorance of the inner workings of the church was dwarfed by a sense of wanting to get it right; after all, this was all new. Little did I know, for years to come, that one line uttered would become my calling card: the church's introduction to its first young Presbyterian convert.

Chapter 12

There were times I sensed heaven so close, I honestly felt life couldn't get any better. Dressed in our finest, the lights turned down and the overhead spotlight illuminating the choir loft filled with high school and college students (a group that featured some remarkable musicians and soloists), I was transported to another dimension of worship. Rather than feeling burdened by conformity, it was as if my favorite song *in the whole wide world* had come on the radio at exactly the right time. Everything wonderful and beautiful regarding life—a warm summer evening with the promise of starlight, the perfect storybook ending to a romantic movie—was captured in moments of elation. I felt as if anything were possible; I felt free. I felt lifted, as if I were on another spiritual plane.

It was hard as a twelve- or thirteen-year-old to be able to relate this newfound experience to family and friends who had known me all my life. Except for how I dressed, I still looked the same, but I could not express to others why my life choices and targeted passions had veered off in another direction. I lived for time spent with my new friends and Sunday night services. My parents must have looked upon this time as similar to my other ventures separate from them. I had basically operated as an only child, because my brother was so much older and already out on his own. I gravitated to hanging with friends who were older or had older siblings and jumped at the chance for sleepovers and invitations to dinner. But this time was different; it did not play itself out so easily.

As time went on, I was torn between my obligation to attend church with my parents and my desire to cultivate stronger ties with my new friends and their way of life. My mother encouraged participation in our home church, and so I found myself rehearsing in the Presbyterian youth choir one Sunday morning before the main service. In early spring, the church's fabulous stained-glass windows allowed a colored ray of sun to warm my face while we sang Cat Stevens' *Morning Has Broken* to the beautiful strains of an acoustic guitar. It was another transportable moment, one in which I could have stayed forever, a sense that this was enough—I could feel the same beautiful flow. However, I believed it wasn't sustainable within the confines of a structured Protestant service, and the pull to submerge myself even deeper into my newfound religion only became stronger. My parents eventually relented; I stopped going to church with them altogether.

The newness of worship gave way to committing more of myself to relationships within the church. Time commitment, prayer commitment, and relational commitments tightened the circle around me without my really noticing; I had formed new attachments, and our times together became of foremost importance. To remain connected, staying "prayed up" was a must. Like within any clique, religious or otherwise, the differences between *us* and *them* became more prominent as my worldview became smaller. My problem was that family was still family, and differences with which I had been comfortable all my life took on an ominous feel, like an ill-fitted suit, when brought to attention.

Chapter 13

The summer 1976 Summer Olympic Games in Montreal, Canada, coincided with the return of my cousin. We hadn't seen each other in years, although she had been living in South Texas. Somehow, I only recall spending time with Diana that summer; Karen must have spent more time with the grandparents. We were in high school; our tastes and activities had changed, but some things remained intact. That ability of hers to make me laugh at her flighty nervousness, her silly anxiety over trying new things, snapped back like a ball and paddle attached by a rubber string. True to form, we had not been stretched too far apart for the connection to break; we went back to our familiar selves.

Diana's appearance did not alarm me personally. She had always kept her fine hair shorn and boyish. (The exception was for one of her elementary school pictures, in which she sported a curly perm. Much to her displeasure, the photo had always been Granny's favorite.) But I was acutely aware of her mannerisms and dress when I took her around my youth group. I figured they just didn't know Diana as I knew her. It was up to me to show others the way I saw her apart from her dress code, which obviously did not reflect the church's *holiness* standards. She was loads of fun and, to boot, had lived out of state.

In the middle of summer, lots of things were going on, and I was not about to sacrifice time apart from my friends, so I dragged her along. I took her to Wednesday night service, which wasn't that big of a stretch for her. She had heard plenty of fiery Baptist sermons, compelling people to the altar at my grandparents' church. In fact, she met our pastor and gave him a thumbs-up for his good and well-delivered sermon. Next on the agenda was the yearly Lions Club carnival, which featured rides such as the Zipper, apart from the arcades and cotton candy.

I was standing in the mid-afternoon sun, watching my cousin act a fool on one of the juvenile rides, when an adult from our church came by and said something that shook me for a moment. Laughingly she remarked that she had told the other young lady riding with my cousin in the little Ferris wheel cage to "be careful!" I instantly knew to what she was referring: Diana's sexual orientation, based on her boyish looks. I immediately defended her: "Oh, she's suffered through a bitter divorce between her parents and has had a hard time because of it. Her mother is a terrible person." "Yeah, I thought she had the appearance of someone who lacked love and supervision," remarked the woman. I continued looking up at my cousin ringing that ridiculous cowbell in the ride's cage, nervously laughing at her exaggerated fear. Suddenly, the bright day dimmed. How many others looked on my cousin as *different* or as a spiritual threat because of her appearance? This was my life-long cousin, and she was funny, by God. Couldn't people see that? She was not anything to be feared—far from it! She was vulnerable.

* * *

That same summer, I hung with a group of older girls, some already out of high school. The only other girl in our group my age was the pastor's daughter. Her only sibling was six years older, so she was accustomed to being around older peers and drew the reputation for being mature for her age. Because of this association, even though we were too young to drive, we never experienced a shortage of friends with wheels. Driving around while listening to tunes either on the radio or through an eight-track player was par for most kids our age. Until I started a summer job the year before my junior year, most of my days were spent going somewhere in a car to get from one moment to another—planned or otherwise. My schedule revolved around my friends' schedules. I quickly left my traditional routine of three meals a day at home to eat out frequently with kids who didn't give much thought to the family table. If somebody needed a full meal in the middle of the afternoon, we were there; I usually just had a Coke.

Another jarring moment occurred that same week while sitting at a table with my cousin and friends in the back dining room of our local Sambo's for a 2:00 p.m. lunch. Our restaurant, like the original Sambo's located in Santa Barbara, California, played up its connection to author Helen Bannerman's *The Story of Little Black Sambo*. Famous for its fluffy pancakes and other traditional café-style menu, it was frequented by many due to its twenty-four-hour availability. I remember when the motifs and murals depicting the picaninny caricatures in the children's book were taken down, and the inside of the restaurant resembled any other diner.

We sat laughing and commenting on social events of the day when the current Olympic Games came up. Immediately the group began whooping and hollering over the East German women swimmers, "Those hulks!" "God, what manly bodies!" "Proud of those flat chests, huh?" and so forth. Of course, this was long before the truth was revealed about an East German systemic, state-orchestrated drug program that propelled their women's swimming team to eclipse the Americans in ten of eleven races, even though the Americans set nine American records in those Olympic events. My cousin, who had sat quietly eating her salad, spoke up in a serious manner, "I'd be proud of myself if I had that much talent and had achieved something as great as an Olympic medal. I'd be very proud." Of course! My cousin played basketball. She was in the ROTC because her dad was in the Air Force.

Mortified, I quickly acted to stifle further comment from her. I leaned over and said, "I think they're just talking about their massive size and height—their resemblance to men, rather than regarding their talent." It was becoming unnervingly apparent that differences between my valued friends and my dear cousin were putting me in an embarrassing spot. To me, my cousin's behavior was nothing out of the ordinary—but, through the eyes of my new alliance, old relations were tricky. I still did not see my cousin any differently than I had before, but certain rumblings in the church regarding terminology that was *known* rather than *understood* by me, were beginning to dominate conversations. What had once felt free and life-asserting was taking on a heavier and punitive tone. With worship came this new sense of responsibility to feel toward others a certain way, as to safeguard against temptations that I knew little about. I was physically and morally sexually innocent, and the dark undertone addressing this "spirit of the world" was something that just wasn't clear to me, yet. In time, it would be made painfully so.

Chapter 14

My first encounter with how the church saw and addressed homosexuality occurred without fully understanding what was going on. I had heard the term from a distance (the news, in magazines, conversations regarding someone else, someplace else), but I had not reached a true comprehension of the word. How could I? I was heavily involved within a church youth group that prided itself on being *in the world but not of the world. Separateness* meant no going to the movies, no Friday night football games, no public swimming pools (the Old Testament forbade mixed bathing), no short sleeves (our shoulders were never exposed), no sex before marriage, etc. My initial innocence, which was a natural extension of my childhood and upbringing by my own family, morphed into a heightened view of sexuality beyond my own experience—a view based solely on the ideology of the church.

One Sunday night, a powerful prayer service evolved during the altar time and focused on a young man I had never seen. As mentioned previously, the prayer time was not limited to the altars at the front of the church; fervent prayer over someone could break out anywhere in the sanctuary. Such was the case this night. I must have either completed my time at the altar (for I was down there after every Sunday night service) or overheard the zealous prayers to have been drawn to this ever-increasing prayer circle toward the back of the sanctuary. Describing prayer in terms of emotional and spiritual zeal to a person who has not experienced this worship style is next to impossible. It includes but is not restricted to "speaking in tongues," the "laying on of hands," "dancing in the spirit," the gift of "tongues and interpretation," and other manifestations of the Holy Ghost.

Theatrical interpretations of *intercessory prayer* on behalf of someone else attempt to convey the passion but are still limited by not being in the moment. George Gershwin's English-language opera, *Porgy and Bess*, featuring an entire cast of classically trained African American singers, includes a powerful scene in which Porgy, the disabled street beggar living in the slums of Charleston, intercedes on behalf of Bess, a woman with a disreputable history. Bess is a woman caught between Crown, her abusive and possessive lover, and Sportin' Life, her drug dealer. Following a church picnic, Bess is raped by her old lover while isolated and alone. Porgy, who has fallen in love with Bess, implores some of the women in town to pray with him for Bess, who is sick and suffering. It is a beautiful scene operatically and choreographically, depicting the group struggling in prayer on behalf of this woman tormented by her addictions.

I could see from the periphery this same type of struggle from individuals closely positioned to the blond-haired man whose hands were raised in fervent, pleading prayer. A much-respected, deeply spiritual man in the congregation stood on the pew behind him in deep travail with his hands placed on the man's shoulders. Another woman, with whom I was acquainted due to her having smaller children whom I adored, was by his side in loud, boisterous petition to God. Our pastor prayed over him; on and on it went. The throng of people prayed with an intensity usually reserved for someone who had strayed and was being prayed back into the fold.

As "victory" began to hold sway over whatever this young man was praying to overcome, a poignant moment caught my eye that immediately identified him as a *prodigal son*. A quiet older woman with tears of joy, hands folded prayerfully, maneuvered herself to stand next to the man. Her lifted gaze, filled with such relief and open adoration, could only be interpreted as that of a mother. This woman, whom I had seen many times, without voicing it, was re-attaching herself to this stranger in our midst. He was obviously no stranger to her, or to others, I would soon learn.

The pastor's daughter, who was standing next to me, leaned over and discreetly said, "He's homosexual." Suddenly, the man had a label and a condition. While the young man was openly being embraced in rejoicing and tearful reunion, the man who had fervently prayed over him looked positively spent, like something had been taken out of him during his determined intercession. The whole experience—though deemed a victorious outcome, one that would carry us through the week until we returned for our next service—left me in questioning awe. My inquisitiveness was not over the wrongness or rightness of homosexuality but rather regarding its spiritual sway. How long had this man been gone, and what had brought him back? This man, who was obviously known by many, who had a close-knit family of father, mother, and adoring sister (whom I had known since coming to church), was a mystery. Who was he, and why had he been a secret for so long?

In the car on the way home, I listened intently as my older friend Sue explained more of the details surrounding this man's past and return. Too young to drive, I rode to and from church regularly with a couple and their two young boys whom I often babysat. (My neighborhood chums Donna and Shelley had moved to Houston two years previously.) "Can you believe the courage and spiritual discernment of Cindy?" Sue asked her husband. Apparently the young man had been attending Sunday night services over the last couple of weeks, and the woman whom I noticed praying beside him, Cindy, had approached him at the end of that evening's service and implored him to pray. "God wants to do something miraculous in your life," she had told him. The man, a stranger to her, had replied, "You don't understand. I've had this sin since I was eight years old." "I don't care what it is. God wants to deliver you." Like me, she didn't know the young man's relationship to the congregation. She had simply noticed a stranger repeatedly returning to sit in the back of the church.

The fascinating conversation regarding homosexuality continued during the car ride. Sue, who had at one time taught nursing at the local junior college, reiterated to her husband and me instruction from her early years of training. "We learned in nursing school that homosexuality was one of the most difficult disorders to cure. Next to impossible." Disorder, psychological diagnosis, sin, abomination—they all addressed the dire condition of our newly known brother and stressed the degree of miracle we had all just witnessed in overcoming such a spiritual death sentence.

This incident marked the beginning of heightened urgency and targeted dialogue within the church regarding sexuality. I would have more questions regarding this spiritual sin and its latest redeemed victim. But as fascinating as newfound knowledge shapes understanding and begins to encroach upon the island of innocence, biased interpretations can bring profound fear and paranoia into unsuspecting young lives. Formative minds can be held captive by zealous, vicious precepts until they are old enough to interpret for themselves matters of spiritual truths—if they're brave enough to question.

Chapter 15

Spirit of the world was the phrase repeatedly used to explain the pervasive, threatening imposition of homosexuality upon the rest of us—particularly those *in the narrow way*. As a sophomore in high school, I was still trying to navigate my own way through a barrage of questions regarding sex ("When is it considered too far with a boy?" "When is *it* going to happen to me?" "How big do my breasts have to be to get a boy to look at me?"). At the same time, I was confronted with an overriding obsession with homosexuality as a force to which everyone would eventually succumb if they did not stay prayed up. Time at church began to be spent more in impromptu prayer vigils rather than actual scheduled services. A heaviness descended upon the place where I had initially experienced such freedom in worship. I attributed this to maturing in the faith after four years of attendance. I was no longer the new kid on the block; I had a responsibility to uphold as an insider.

Staying prayed up was vital to one's social standing within the community of faith. I had witnessed adults, who did not manage to *pray through* during an excitable altar call, be systematically marginalized within the ranks of the church. Praying through was hard work—unlike the Baptist altar calls where one showed up with repentant tears either to sign a card or "rededicate" their lives to Jesus in whatever form that took. Praying through was the task of confronting whatever was holding one back from the design of God and/or the church for one's life. It was somehow deemed complete when the people praying alongside witnessed a total surrender of will. There was weeping repentance, dancing in the spirit, speaking in tongues, or simply a sense of breaking through some sort of personal wall to a place of contrite deliverance that was agreed upon by those praying in earnest. When it happened in the moment, a joyful expression of worship swept like a wave over those participating. But this did not always happen on the first trip to the altar or prayer room. This might take several times at the altar of prayer, allowing a time for introspection and often, isolation—mandated by the mindset of the people rather than the individual. And much woe fell on the person during this struggle.

Being cut off from the congregation was bad enough, but church members also curtailed all interactions with others closely known to the individual for fear of contamination and spread. Families were often disrupted—and, in some cases, split for good—due to irreparable spiritual differences that could not be resolved within the church community. Old and New Testament sources were held up in defense of these temporary and sometimes permanent separations between mother and father, children and parents, grandparents, extended family, and the best of friends. Unlike the Old Testament story of David (before he was deemed king of Israel) and his best friend Jonathan, who made a covenant of friendship despite Jonathan's father's murderous pursuit of David, congregants often severed friendships in the name of preserving themselves against the wiles of the devil.

In the midst of this upheaval and pernicious gossip regarding whose spiritual integrity was up next for scrutiny ("Guess who's out of whack?" was an expression that identified the target), our youth group carried on with its usual close-knit shenanigans as best we could. We drove around in cars listening to our favorite eight-tracks, unmindful of seat belts or the limit of people who could fit in the backseat. We buzzed the Sonic on our bikes; we drove waitresses crazy by our tables of endless requests for refills on Coke and Dr Pepper. We played tennis; we sang; we papered houses; we daydreamed over boys or girls we could never have. We remained youthful but ties increasingly became strained and cut as our friends' parents and grandparents became the subject of division—those who directly or indirectly challenged the man in the pulpit . . . or his wife.

As the fear of homosexuality-by-association began to spread, many innocent youth center get-togethers, choir rehearsals, or youth prayer services turned into psychological scare fests that often left a person accused. These young teens would be stranded, isolated, and left alone to figure out for themselves their path back to God's grace and their circle of peers. Some never did. Either by outright denial and refusal to conform to the church's accusations or by an extended exile that left them doubt-filled and fearful, they walked or ran away. Of course, some of the heated prayer sessions had more to do with who was being loyal to the church and who was acting as a "spy within the camp" rather than outright accusations of homosexuality. But the overriding premise still held that homosexuality was an evil spirit, one that would invade people if they were unwilling to engage in spiritual warfare against it.

Those of us who survived these prayer sessions, who managed our minds and spirits not to "sympathize with the devil," held onto our standing within the youth group by willfully choosing not to associate with those who had left. Impromptu meetings in the halls at school or within community settings proved trying and uncomfortable, but we held firm (sadly) out of fear rather than loyalty. Those closely associated with the church's exiled were not the only ones who were in danger of guilt by association. Distant, contoured, intertwined relationships that could be somehow traced back to a person in question similarly served as reason for suspicion. "Weren't you seen with Brenda?" "You chose to go to the lake with two friends Saturday afternoon. Isn't that right? Yes, well, the brother of one of those girls' dates Regina, and her great-aunt is Sister Mary." *Gasp.* Mary was one of the church's separated adversaries, labeled a "mocker in the last time" (Jude 1:18, King James Version). I was guilty as charged. A trip to the altar or prayer room until victory was won over allowing the devil a foothold against the Holy Ghost was warranted, if, at sixteen, I still wanted access to my most-valued circle of friends.

Bad dreams began: a sweaty sense of fear upon awakening for school after a long night as the condemned, isolated person at the altar surrounded by vultures in saintly robes. Yet no figurative creatures or representations encircled me, only the faces of people I faithfully worshipped with three times a week.

Chapter 16

Fifth grade: a time of friendship and rivalry, when imagination and reality sometimes still intersect. Not quite old enough to understand all adult references but innocent enough to attach their own interpretation unabashedly, fifth graders are certainly aware of opposite attraction. This narrative depicts my most turbulent elementary school year overshadowed by the fact *the teacher did not like me*. But I was determined to persevere, because, for one whole week, I wore the ID bracelet of a boy in my class I had long admired, before being jilted for another girl of his social status. I was oblivious to such divisions—those people just lived in bigger houses on nicer streets was all.

Competition involved not only which girl liked which boy but extended to which girl befriended which girl, whose picture was best displayed, whose team won, whose report was best received, and who wore it best, now that some of us had started secretly shaving our legs. When we were given a collage project in our illustrious, fully-fledged art class, which rotated weekly with our music class, we enthusiastically tore fashion examples of the early 1970s from our mothers' magazines. We were at least of an age to appreciate current trends.

My nemesis in the fifth grade, Lesa, secured the best picture from the art room's stack of periodicals to paste on her board and later decoupage: a large Coppertone ad featuring a model in a yellow bikini. The tall blond sported a perfect tan that was a result of using the product. At age eleven, we figured the body came with it as well. So smitten by the picture, the rest of the girls in class began a diligent search for more bathing suit ads, which proved difficult since we were in the middle of winter. I managed to find a body lotion ad that pictured a woman wrapped in a fluffy white towel, seated, applying the product to her legs presumably after bathing. It wasn't as centerfold worthy as Lesa's Coppertone model, but it found its place among the other girls on my board wearing the mod, Twiggy-inspired fashions of the day: plaid short dress suits, accents of bulky patented heels and bowler hats.

I took great pride in my collage board, decked out in the women and colors of 1970. I enthusiastically drizzled Elmer's glue over the entire piece for added texture, as we had been instructed, and shellacked the surface with the toxically aromatic varnish supplied by the art room for a finished, artistic touch. My original trendy art piece resided in the closet for years after it was displayed in my room, until it was thrown out (by my mother!) during one of our home's episodic cleanouts. This event occurred without my knowing, for I had outgrown cutting pictures from magazines just like I'd moved on from our old Betsy McCall paper doll days.

* * *

In the icy winter of 1977, my growing fear of my own Siberia culminated in a self-fulfilled prophecy, harbored and fed by my dreams. At seventeen, like so many others before me, I found myself abandoned at a Pentecostal altar due to a "bad spirit." There was no other way to explain the coldness that had invaded another impromptu prayer meeting on a Sunday afternoon in the middle of a rare snow and ice storm that blanketed our town for better part of a week.

I had accompanied my two closest friends to pray for a young couple whose marriage was crumbling as a result of the wife's succumbing to an evil spirit. My two friends were heavily invested in the couple: the wife was one friend's sister, and my other friend's sister was married to the wife's brother. Our pastor, his wife, and some other prayer warriors gathered in the sanctuary to pray over this situation before the evening service, which was always heavily attended. At some point during the rising vocal prayers offered on bent knees around the long wooden altars, attention turned to me. I felt something was wrong. The adults zeroed in on me while the joyous tide turned in favor of the young wife, who had begun "running in the spirit" in the aisles of the church. I was as cold as ice and could not figure out why, other than I hadn't stayed prayed up and had allowed the devil a foothold by succumbing to fear of the situation over which we were praying. This particular woman had been the subject of many prayer sessions because of a suspected "spirit of homosexuality" within her family; she had come forth, confessing she had been molested by her mother for years.

Unable to connect with the apparent victory of the young woman skipping and praising God through the church, I began to feel isolated, fearful, and somewhat resentful of how the scales of judgment had tipped. Suddenly, she slammed into one of the wooden pillars of the church's arches that were strategically placed at the ends of the front, middle, and back pews on either side of the sanctuary. With her eyes closed during a final spiritual victory lap, she had landed her two front teeth in the non-giving structure and snapped them in two. As others rushed to her, I raised my head from the altar and said, "That was my fault." The pastor's wife, whose dark irises were indistinguishable from her pupils, glared directly into my eyes and said, "Yes, it was." I left the sanctuary that afternoon desperate and alone, determined to come back that night and pray for deliverance during the night end's altar call.

I wasted no time after the sermon and ended up on my knees in approximately the same spot I had occupied earlier that day, with the entire church surrounding me exactly like in the dreams that had begun haunting me. Here I was, at the intersection of dark imagination and reality, under the spotlight within the night service's dimmed lighting. Silhouetted against the darkness were faces of those who had once admired my faithfulness. I saw Sunday school teachers drop their heads in sadness at my predicament, simultaneously keeping their prayerful distance. The priority appeared not to be my deliverance but, rather, that my open conviction would serve as a warning to others. The young wife, groomed and refreshed since the earlier prayer session, appeared at my side. Encouraged by the *pastoring* adults, she knelt close, looked me in the eyes, and proclaimed, "I'm not afraid of you, devil. I'm not afraid of you." Her statement of bravery was applauded with affirmative shouts from the surrounding faithful.

I left the church on foot, cloaked in darkness, making my way across lawns drifted in snow. I crossed the street a couple of blocks down from my old Presbyterian church and headed for home, far on the other side of town. Approximately a mile from my house, a church couple with their young son spotted me walking through a parking lot, stopped, and picked me up. They delivered me safely home, but I sensed the spiritual distance they had to keep. In retrospect, I suspect it dawned on someone that it might not reflect well on the church to have one of its young female parishioners, who had caught a ride to church that night due to icy conditions, walking the streets alone after 10:00 p.m. No one had called out or followed me into the cold night.

I endured the longest week of all my years in school from that Sunday night to the following. The first two days of the school week were declared snow days due to ice accumulation on the roads. That didn't stop me from driving in desperation to the other side of town, temporarily stalling out on the ice on my way, to pray at the church's altar. My father was upset I had driven my car in the bad weather; therefore, the next day, I asked him for a ride to church. By dusk, another prayer group had assembled around me that prayed into the night, until my father impatiently arrived at the back entrance of the church to take me home. Knowing my father had no understanding of what was going on, it was up to me to face him with a somewhat controlled demeanor, rather than exhibit my hysteria over facing eternal damnation not just down the road, but in the immediacy, for my evil ways. He could not understand what needed praying over for so long and was equally irritated at the late hour on a school night. Good points—only I didn't see the situation that way. My parents did not understand the spiritual implications. I was further isolated, being unyoked from them.

I managed to make it to my part-time job and school the rest of the week, skipping the Wednesday night service and steering as clear as I could from my church friends in the high school halls, because I was regarded as *off-limits*. By Saturday, I was desperate. I had my mother drive me to the church mid-afternoon to pray but not before she stopped at a drive-in to get some lunch. While trying to explain my painful inability to reach God and reconnect with a church that had become my way of life, I watched the helpless tears of my mother fall into the sandwich she was eating. Nevertheless, she took me to the church for another prayer session gathered on my behalf that did not go well.

I struggled all night at home and kept my parents up with tearful anxiety over losing my soul to an evil spirit. At one point I laid the Bible open on our kitchen table and pointed to a verse that I believed was speaking of me: "And others save with fear, pulling *them* out of the fire; hating even the garment spotted by the flesh." Jude verse 24. Sometime before dawn, my father took his church clothes out of the closet, put them on, and called my pastor from the phone in the hall. I stood looking out my bedroom window with such unease that only the headlights of his car coming down our street could appease the painful anxiety that had overtaken me. My intervention was coming.

My pastor, already dressed in his suit for Sunday service, sat in our living room across from my mom and me on the couch, and my father seated on the piano bench. He tried his best to explain to a couple of Presbyterians the context of prayer and guidance from the Holy Ghost that had isolated me as being out of step with God. And then he illuminated us with what was troubling me: the *spirit of homosexuality*. I was a homosexual—someone who at seventeen had kissed maybe three boys, two during a game of spin-the-bottle. What was a homosexual, exactly?

He went on to explain that this was something that apparently had grasped hold of me at a young age. "A couple in our church recently attended a garage sale in town and came across a board decorated with nothing but pictures of girls. The entire piece was covered in women, some wearing minimal clothing. Curious, they turned it over and found Sherry's name on the back. Now, *why* would a young girl be so intrigued with the bodies of women instead of other things children should be interested in?"

Just before my pastor left our home, he went over and comforted my father, who was openly weeping on the piano bench. "Now, now, I'm a father of a teenager myself." After he left, my mother, in her unassuming, contemplative, soft voice commented, "I can see why a young girl cuts out pictures of women she admires. She thinks they're pretty, and they remind her of who she wished she looked like." "No, no, Mom, this is serious. He knows," I said, not wanting my parents to doubt the authority of the pastor on my account. I went to get ready for church, hoping I could get *right* at the altar, now that I knew what the problem was.

Chapter 17

I did in fact *pray through* that night and other nights as well during my last two years of high school. Finally, following a Wednesday night's service, the church leaders decided that I was filled with "too worldly of a spirit" to fit in with the youth of the church. In an extremely rare move, my pastor called my parents at home, imploring them to come to his study immediately following the service to discuss the situation. I didn't even get the chance to answer an altar call.

The pastor recounted to my parents how, during a spring break trip with his family, I had looked on with fascination at the obvious drug culture occurring among young people on the beaches of Padre Island in South Texas. My father asked, "Were they actually doing drugs?" My pastor went on to explain that I exhibited a "spirit of the world" laced with doubt and fear that continually caused me to question, and they could not allow this to influence the rest of the kids in the church. I appeared anxiously desperate to everyone in the room. Attempting to understand this thought process, my mother brought up the fact that perhaps all this talk of bad spirits and such had put these fearful thoughts in my head. In response to this honest observation made by my mother to better understand these accusations, the pastor's wife rose in swift defense of her husband: "Our kids don't even attend the movies, much less football games, dances, or other activities that would expose them to such behaviors. How dare you blame the church for planting these ideas in her head!"

The conversation represented the last straw over something I had done, said, or over an intruding evil thought I had let sway my faith. As I returned to the sanctuary, I nearly tripped over a group of people sitting in the dark outside the pastor's study door (trying to overhear what was going on inside). My parents had exited the other door that opened into the hall. The group looked up expectantly as I went to retrieve my purse from where I had been sitting. I softly uttered, "Goodbye," not quite fully realizing this would be the last time I would set foot in that church. Ever.

And so, during the last month of my senior year, I was ushered into a world I hadn't really been a part of for the past six years: from the awkward beginnings of my adolescence to the end of high school. Thankfully, I still had other friends due to my class time and job through Health Occupation Students of America, including my coworkers at the hospital where I was employed. The last month of classes were spent dodging stares and chance encounters with my former youth group in the school's hallways. On graduation night, instead of attending the anticipated celebration for our church's graduating seniors usually held at one of our regional lake's resorts, I left with a new bunch of friends headed for a lake beach party.

A couple of weeks before graduation, I had driven to a spot on the lake to comfort myself, now exiled from my usual attendance at Sunday night service. It was all I had known for years; I now found myself in unknown territory. It was as though I had been away for a long time. I was out of place and felt unprepared for a big world that I had been taught to avoid. I was sitting in the sand, looking out on the large expanse of water, when I heard cars drive up on the bluff behind me and people exit excitedly. They were carrying coolers and towels for a Sunday beach get-together at dusk. I panicked. I gathered my stuff and ran up a path on the other side of some trees to avoid being seen. I reached the safety of my car and drove quickly away from a scene played out routinely on many beachfronts in the early evening fade of a weekend. But a Sunday night gathering outside the familiar church walls felt as ominous as the approaching "last days" of reproachful man. I had left the sanctity of God's graciousness, to which I felt there was no return. I was now alone and scared.

***

Another Friday night high school graduation followed the weekend of mine. Diana Lynn Shields paraded down the center aisle of the Tom Bean High School basketball gym in her bright orange robe to my approving applause. That thing about my being born first held true: we were the same class year, but I finished ahead of her by a week.

The summer before our junior year of high school, Diana and her family returned to Tom Bean. My uncle had retired from the Air Force after his last post in San Antonio. He had purchased a piece of land down the road from our grandparents' farmhouse where we had played as children. On another sunny Friday, my cousins gathered with their dad, stepmom, and stepsister to watch a semi, pulling their trailer home, navigate the crossing of a deep culvert between them and their home's new destination. The bottom of the trailer hit the ditch and nearly split in two. My uncle sank to his knees, for he had given the order to cross, while Diana and Karen, true to their nature, started screaming and crying like banshees. My mother witnessed the whole thing; I arrived shortly after the big bang with the intention of welcoming everybody back home.

The trailer home was eventually patched up, and the blended family set about the routine of work, school, and readjustment to small-town civilian life. (My aunt was no longer in the picture; she remained in Nevada with her old lover.) But the distance between my cousins and me was much farther than the geological mileage between our homes; we had all changed.

Diana was still attempting to play basketball despite significant knee trauma she had sustained while playing in San Antonio. She also got involved with the agriculture program at school and began readying a steer to enter at a livestock show before the poor creature was zapped by lightning right outside her window. Karen was busy adapting to new surroundings and dealing with the isolation of being left out by Diana and Glenda. Adolescent tempers and hormones flared, causing discord between Karen and her stepmom. This, sadly, led to a division between the two sisters as well.

For a short while after graduation, we enjoyed some brief, celebratory encounters regarding our completion. We both set about dealing with life after high school by either keeping or obtaining jobs. My school co-op job employed me full time in the hospital lab, and Diana got a job as a nurses' aide in the same hospital. We waved, smiled, and went on our way. I had fallen in love over the summer and enrolled in the local junior college for the fall semester; Diana took a new position at the Johnson & Johnson plant in town, working second shift. Glenda married the following summer and had a baby within a year. Karen had left long before, returning to her mother in Reno, waving bye-bye to the lone water tower of Tom Bean. She returned for a couple of brief visits interspaced by the funeral of our granddad, followed by Granny's fifteen years later.

Diana and I continued living in the same area, only seeing each other on family occasions until I went looking for her one day. I needed a roommate for an undetermined length of time due to an unexpected turn of events. I could use some familiar company and help with the rent.

Prior to our moving in together, the last time I remembered the cousins' gathering for any length of time was outside their home just after our graduations. Under the stars while sitting on lawn chairs and the tailgate of a pickup, our conversation and cutting up turned to progressive views of the day. I listened, unsurprised, to Karen make supportive remarks regarding homosexuality, undeterred by others' comments. It was all in fun; we were relaxed and trying to one-up each other with our opinions and reported facts. Although I was freshly ousted from the church, I was still on point with its teaching. I believed that, to secure my eternal salvation, there would be a necessary return at some point. So, I ended our little debate with a smug observation: "Well, homosexuality will end itself on its own accord. Couples won't be able to have children. That takes care of that."

Part 3

What I Had Always Known

Chapter 18

On December 9, 1980, I awoke to my bedside clock radio's alarm announcing the overnight death of John Lennon. My cousin told me later that day that the same news had awakened her. Talk of his assassination reverberated around the workplace and eventually Christmas gatherings, but the significance of the event faded into the background of my own current events.

Diana had moved into the bungalow house I was renting by mid-November. My husband of little over a year had left following our November ninth anniversary dinner (within three months he would be hospitalized in a Veterans Administration hospital, suffering from a chronic mental disorder). Later in the month, I nearly passed out while getting ready to attend my family's Thanksgiving dinner. I confirmed my pregnancy the following week at the lab where I worked.

We settled into the routine of one of my darkest winters. Every morning for the next four months, I awakened my cousin sleeping in the room adjacent to the bathroom with the sound of retching while brushing my teeth. By that time of the morning it would have been the second time I had vomited before leaving for my early hospital shift. But I continued working, and Diana continued her two part-time jobs, bitching about the management of the diner where she served lunch. Her financial contribution toward rent helped me dig my way out of debt from some unthrift spending on the part of my husband, including an outrageous phone bill.

Though we had not been around each other for any extended length of time in years, we mostly functioned within a framework of familiarity. Our petty disagreements and aggravations (she wanted to use a fresh towel for every bath; I wanted to hang them for reuse since they were bridal shower gifts) had more to do with habits and misinterpretations handed down by the adults in our shared family. They had aired grievances and attached labels to those sharing our same heritage in the presence of "little pitchers." While growing up, we had often overheard our parents discuss others. She saw me as spoiled or as always getting my way, because I enjoyed a gentler upbringing. I saw her as being played by a stereotypic view fostered by jealousies—particularly when she assumed that she knew all the facts. Nevertheless, we held onto shared memories and a sense of trust. During a challenging time, we provided a home for one another: a listening ear when needed or individual space when desired.

Diana understood the seriousness of my current living situation, the bearings on my future, but she never pried. She had not come to our wedding and had only limited contact with my husband. Likewise, her friends and personal pursuits were her own. Outside of a party she threw for a couple of close friends one night, I knew little about her personal acquaintances. I knew she had adult relations and thought nothing of it when she told me a long-distance boyfriend was coming through town for the weekend and wanted to stay with her. No problem.

I arrived home late after the pair had returned from going out and tiptoed past their sleeping forms. Lights were out, and I, stupidly or perhaps passively, went to bed without closing my door. I awoke sometime in the night to the rhythmic sounds of passion. I lay perfectly silent in the dark and gratefully managed to fall back to sleep almost immediately, because I had to be at work early Saturday morning. I returned after my morning shift and wondered where Diana's friend was. Before she was to leave for work, she came into my room to talk, downcast over his leaving. When she had pressed him about sticking around longer so they could enjoy the anticipated weekend together, he basically admitted he had stopped in for the night and was merrily hitting the road without a commitment of return. "I'm tired of this," she said. "I feel like I'm nothing but a bus stop for him, where he comes and goes as he pleases." My situation wasn't much better, but I felt bad for her. I couldn't help thinking how humiliating it must have been for her to relay her feelings of being used, particularly after I had been awakened by her enjoyment. But she had always exhibited blunt truthfulness, despite her wild, scaredy-cat reactions as a child. I watched her leave for work, noticing the cold damp grayness outside.

The fact that she felt confident confiding in me confirmed our childhood bond. Even in a trying situation, a distinctive character trait or event would embody times we had previously enjoyed, and I found myself laughing with the Diana I remembered, mired within our adult constraints.

One spring evening, while both of us were attempting to hang a large picture, we disturbed my husband (home for a short while between hospitalizations) from his troubled sleep. Emerging from the bedroom in obvious distress, he cried, "Baby, what are y'all doing?" My cousin stuck the head of the hammer into her mouth as if to hide evidence. "We're just trying to get this up on the wall," I replied, trying to suppress my laughter. Until that moment I had not realized how much I missed our silly childhood escapades.

Change was inevitable. She signed up for a photography course at the local junior college after purchasing an expensive camera. Soon, there was an open textbook in the house and homework due. She moved out a couple of months before I delivered at the end of a hot July. By early fall I had set up house in an apartment across town as a newly singled parent. Over the next three years, Diana completed her associate's degree, joined the Navy, and headed for her initial assignment in Mississippi after completing Naval basic training. It would be another hot, eventful summer before we would meet again and confer on how much we and the world around us had changed.

Chapter 19

The early '80s were busy and invigorating for me. I had successfully transitioned into mainstream living outside the walls of the church. I had divorced and was carving out an independent life with my son. I was promoted at work after obtaining a certification in histology and was taking another stab at higher education. Eschewing the opportunity afforded immediately after high school, I had basically blown off the first year at our local junior college with a dropped class and my first D ever, in pursuit of a romantic attachment. Reading newspaper excerpts regarding my classmates' destination weddings, college degrees, and job appointments left me uneasy regarding my self-designated place behind the eight ball. So, I began night school after my full-time day job, taking full advantage of two sets of grandparents' availabilities for childcare during evening classes.

Though the times were lean and the schedule sometimes grueling, delightful surprises along the way revealed a world that had before been slightly out of reach. A beautiful young woman became a close friend, filling the void of a sister I never had but always wanted. Gail was six years older than I and was the wife of a colleague in the hospital lab where I worked. I was enthralled by her striking features, family background, and her medical history: she was a cancer survivor.

Her upper face resembled a young Linda Ronstadt with large dark almond-shaped orbs, while her lower face with its distinctively upturned nose evoked Sally Fields. That accent—a fusion of Houston, southern Oklahoma, Northeast Texas, and SMU—was uniquely all hers. She had come from a completely different background and lived a much different life than my own, which I welcomed as a fresh change. Her beginning was as bizarre as anything I had ever heard. She was handpicked as an infant, on account of her big brown eyes, from an orphanage in the Bronx by her fighter-pilot father returning to the States in the middle of the 1953 Brooklyn Dodgers and Yankees World Series. Her family's professional jobs and degrees, as well as the pain of her parents' divorce and the suicide of her adopted father that followed, molded her childhood. Her mother eventually remarried upon the awaited approval from Gail. Her new stepfather's family business afforded them some of the finer things in life. She also benefitted from his outright spoiling, designed to win over the headstrong girl.

By the time I came into the picture, she had already undergone several different rounds of chemo and radiation for Hodgkin's Lymphoma; she had been diagnosed at twenty-two. Though she would succumb to what she called "this sucking disease" thirteen years after her diagnosis, she would put up a hell of a fight. The scarring of her body, debilitating nausea and vomiting, the inability to have children, a painful divorce, and hair loss over and again were just a few of the obstacles she faced. Yet along the way she also managed to chart her own course, remarry, and retain a sense of style few around her could pull off. She was stubborn and defiant when it came to decisions being pushed on her too quickly but vulnerable and distant when it came to relationships that threatened her sense of self-protection. From childhood until her death she viewed her adopted self as *rejected*, and it would color her perception at every unexpected turn. As protective as she was over self, she was an advocate for others, long before being so was as accepted as it is today. One day she took me to task over the spiritual dogma that continued to color *my* perception of the world.

It was no secret to me that Gail enjoyed the companionship of her openly gay colleagues in the respiratory/cardiology department where she worked. She thought it hilarious when, after running into a flamboyant work cohort, he began twirling in the middle of a department store aisle, asking for her superb opinion regarding his multi-colored scarves. Tom, her husband, shuffled uncomfortably, which humored Gail as well. Although she knew some of my background within the church and hints of its extreme fundamentalism, she did not realize how deep-seated those taught beliefs were.

During a family vacation in which Gail accompanied us, she and I found ourselves in a determined debate. Gail and I had spent the morning shopping, followed by venturing out on our own in search of a historic home I had remembered from previous childhood trips. Beneath the Russian Villa residence on a high bluff overlooking the historical section of Hot Springs, Arkansas, we argued over my judgmental view of gays. The sin of homosexuality was an abomination, clearly stated, case closed. Much to Gail's consternation, I could not allow myself to be weakened in the face of her relational ties or with examples of other gays we knew in the community. I could not convey to her that it was a fear of judgment unto myself, and so I stood firm. She became frustrated to the point of throwing up her arms, declaring she could not believe my willingness to swallow and hold onto such a closed view. We managed to patch up the tension-defined distance by taking a picture and moving on, each secretly vowing never to return to the subject. But another encounter would shake me to the core and once again challenge the deliberate tainting by others and lay open my fears.

In the summer following her Naval basic training, my cousin Diana returned to Texas to visit family, primarily her father and stepmom, before reporting to her first assignment. My uncle Denny had taken a job as the groundskeeper and security detail at the lake campus of the university I was to start in the fall. The private beach of Austin College is located on the most northern point of the Texas side of Lake Texoma. It had been my playground for years; since high school, I never missed a chance to lie on its shores during the peak seasonal months, dreaming of the day I would own my own boat. One Saturday afternoon, while sharing a cooler of soft drinks and a tube of Bain de Soleil tanning gelée with a good friend, I watched my cousin stroll down from her father's job-appointed home to say hi. Hi, after hardly any contact following the few months we lived together. Though the view had changed, we both certainly welcomed it.

She wore a white t-shirt, khaki shorts, and the shortest hair of her life, shorn above her ears and hairline in the back. She talked excitedly about her new life and friends in the military. She was eager to get to her new post. She spoke of the strict routine and morning punctuality that had prompted her to cut her hair and keep it as short as possible, which I immediately filed away as *sensible*. She talked openly of her stepmom's disapproval of her progressive attitude, which I again interpreted as not liking her butch haircut and way of dress. Although my friend was taken aback by Diana's masculine appearance, clearly buffed-up by her physical training, I took consolation in the fact that Diana was greatly offended at being labeled a lesbian simply because she had signed up for the Navy. "I told those guys, who called us a bunch of dykes, it's a funny thing that, when trouble comes, you call on us." It was good to talk to her under the afternoon sun, and we vowed to meet later that night at a local club.

Saturday night in Texoma Land meant a bar blaring live dance music, primarily of country persuasion, but with a little rock thrown in for the '70s crowd. Diana was already set up with a couple of friends by the time we got there. One of her male friends on leave from the Army was sporting a "high and tight" haircut, compliments of the military due to some prior misbehavior on his part. The Seven and Sevens were flowing, and the soldier and sailors were laughing outright over how lame civilians partied. My friend from the lake and I joined right in.

During the conversation I learned Diana was in for only a few days longer. Within the following week, she planned to meet up with some of her friends from Basic for a final goodbye before they all went to their designated posts. Sounded like fun to me! I offered to go along, so we could spend a little more time together before she left for Mississippi. She responded casually that she didn't think the *progressive* slant of the club in Dallas would be to my liking. Feeling relaxed by the flowing drink and loud music I absentmindedly mumbled, "Why would you want to go *there*?" With her side-tipped grin and a direct look she replied, "You're not that dumb, Sherry."

I felt like I had just been kicked in the gut. The fogginess in my head from the drink cleared immediately, as did the haze before my eyes. All that I had known and believed lay exposed, withering and dying. Memories of my acceptance of her dress and ways as just being *who she was* now had ugly titles attached: gay, lesbian, homosexual. The excuses I had evoked to my friends and sister-in-law came back like a cold, watery slap: *"Hey, Stupid!"* "Yeah, but she can dress any way she wants; she's got that huge set of boobs. I wish I had half as much as she has." As if having boobs had anything to do with being straight or gay.

The night within the bar carried on as usual for all the other patrons—except me. A cloud of distance enveloped, moving me emotionally and physically away from the group, from the music and my cousin. She seemed oblivious to my epiphany. Later in the night she asked why I wasn't hanging with everybody and having fun. I made up an excuse about needing to call it a night after spending the day in the sun. That night, I left knowing there would be no phone calls clarifying a meet-up time for another rendezvous before her departure. In fact, I wouldn't see her again until a year or two later during the Christmas holidays, when she made a point to come see me while visiting my parents. She introduced us to her new friend and roommate from

Mississippi, her partner, though she gracefully avoided that title in front of the family. She needn't have bothered on my account; she looked on her friend during conversation with the same look I recalled over a cup of hot chocolate pretending to be coffee in our childhood game of soap opera. She was in love. The sunlight filtering through the patio sliding glass doors punctuated a truth that had been there all along.

Chapter 20

Time flies, retrospectively. Yet when your nose is to the grindstone in pursuit of a distant dream, time seems to crawl. Then perhaps one day you find yourself living the life you worked toward, only to discover that, no matter how fulfilling or rewarding, it never quite matches up to the dream.

Higher education afforded me the opportunity of medical school, residency, and practice; it also paved the way for relationships and a new family. Whereas my son and I had been two, one more made three; within four years of this union, we were a family of five. Life was full, joyous, busy, and fun-filled but not without its challenges. Growing up brings adolescence and discovery; a profession brings commitments and calendar restraints, while babies bring lack of sleep and yearnings to keep them small and by our side. Into this mix crept a major depressive episode that had been undetectably pursuing me . . . until a black hole suddenly opened one day.

Perhaps I had unknowingly set my own trap, or perhaps it was time to wipe the slate clean and start over. For whatever reason, one day while pumping gas my questioning thoughts regarding God's ability to look upon the cruel acts of life, seemingly with disregard, led me into a two-month wilderness. The enveloping darkness necessitated clinic visits, medication, my mother's extended stay, and deep introspection. Questions, lots of questions—many unanswerable but constant—kept my mind racing and fatigued.

It was inevitable that during this period of facing my eventual, earned damnation, the *church* would loom on this darkening horizon as palpable and relevant as it had been at seventeen. I was back trudging in the cold, shut out and without hope. I reverted to what I had done when young and desperate, trying to plead my case: I woke up my old pastor with a phone call at 7:00 a.m., miles and years from when we had last spoken. His voice sounded as gentle as it had when I was twelve. After briefly reacquainting, I got down to revealing deep fears. He, in turn, without the judgment I so dreaded, spoke gently and encouragingly, even arming me with a bit of scripture that was the opposite of what I was expecting. "No, you can't give up," he said firmly but without harshness. The call ended peaceably. For a moment I felt relief over the condemnation that did not occur. But during our conversation he remembered an accurate detail: "Seems I recall in counseling with you, as a young girl, that you were always wrestling with these questions." I wearily replied, "Yes, I'm still the same. Nothing's changed."

The questions and wrestling with mind and universe continued, interrupted only briefly by personal insights or encouragement from others, until once again in desperation I dialed the same parsonage phone, seeking reassurance. This time his wife picked up, for he was out of town. Regarded as the intimidating spiritual force of the church, she was the last person from whom I expected absolution, but it came in a totally unexpected exchange.

The church had eventually come under fire from former church members who had been targeted. Awareness of the brewing situation had been raised through the local media. The newspaper's reporting had zeroed in on her as much as her husband. Court grievances were filed, and things had gotten ugly before people moved on to the next story.

She discussed what she had been through and, without knowing, gave me permission to take medication—something with which I had been struggling. "You know how I was attacked," she related. "The only way I got through without losing my mind was by leaning on a particular Bible verse. . . . But, who's to say, I may have been better off taking medication." Right before we hung up, she gave me the pardon I was subconsciously seeking. "So, you don't think I'm evil?" I asked, with all the sincerity of a fallen soul. "If you were evil, why would you be calling me? You know we stand for righteousness." It was a common sense, light-bulb-turned-on moment, but, more importantly, I heard it from someone who had passed judgment on me years ago. She, who at one time I had revered as a spiritual counselor, confirmed that my dark night was not a result of being evil. Even though my depression raged on for six more weeks, I had made peace with these two people after twenty years.

* * *

My depression cleared me from the church's sentence regarding hell over heaven. I was no longer held hostage by the grim reminder of an awaiting eternal punishment. I no longer woke in the middle of the night in terror of my family, friends, and myself burning in a *lake of fire throughout infinity* over not being properly baptized, over never having spoken in tongues, over the inability or the unwillingness to live a pure life minute by minute, hour by hour, day by day. I was freed from a dogma that had ensnared me for two decades while I pretended I was as others.

Liberation happened during the night's journey, as I implored, contemplated, and sought the God of my childhood. It happened while reconnecting to the steadfast love of my mother and her simple wisdom of not being able to explain everything. It happened over the simple sharing of a cup of hot tea when she could no longer offer words. It happened while reading written cards from friends and acquaintances. It happened under the care of a therapist and an aging psychiatrist who wasn't afraid to question institutional teachings, which, "like wheat shafts without deep roots, become marred in the muck, unable to stand grounded and tall." I was now free to question without fear.

Chapter 21

Summer 2005, our family moved from South Texas back to my roots in North Texas. My oldest son, a private first class in the Marine Corps, was serving in Iraq. My husband was beginning a new practice, and I was leaving one behind to transition our children into a new neighborhood and school; the youngest had just turned three. My parents now lived an hour away, while my husband's parents remained behind with the company of his brother's family. We were so busy meeting new friends, attending backyard barbecues while checking out churches and mechanics that I didn't feel the full blow of culture shock until eight months in. I hit a wall that was probably best understood by my fifth-grade daughter, who was painfully reminded daily of all she had left behind. She did not fit in.

Life moved on. Boy came home from the war, followed by marriage and a new baby, while kids at home climbed the ladders of kindergarten, elementary, and junior high. Then one day my mother called to say, "My carpal tunnel procedure has been put off for heart surgery, big heart surgery."

Mother's open-heart procedure to repair an aneurysm of her aortic arch and repair or replace her aortic valve, if necessary, occurred the morning of September 4, 2007, following Labor Day weekend. After a harrowing six-week ride in the hospital that included a prolonged stint on the ventilator, unexpected bleeding, and a heart arrhythmia, she succumbed to a blood clot and died at 4 a.m., October 14. Just like that, all sense of normalcy, what was supposed to happen, and the what-ifs paled against a sudden finality we could not seem to process. This was the shock-and-awe period through which I had helped other families transition during my tenure as a palliative-care pediatrician before our move—except this time was different. This time it was me, and I did not know how to transition.

The day-to-day trudge through the grieving period, which I had forecasted (naively) at six weeks, turned totally wacko just shy of the four-month mark. From then to the end of the second year, it was an all-out roller-coaster ride, with my family's trying to cope with "what's happened to Mom" versus Mom's trying to escape from family she sometimes wished she never had. Mom became obsessed beyond reason with glam-rock star Todd Rundgren, whose '70s music she remembered but had never purchased. Mom felt the need to get away: Colorado trip, New York trip, multiple New York trips. Mom wanted to start over from her twenties and live it just a little edgier. Mom changed the way she dressed, the style and color of her hair. So, by April, a friend suggested a certain book might be helpful, and Mom went to the public library in search of Julia Cameron.

In her book, *The Artist's Way,* Julia challenges readers to find their "greater selves" by opening themselves to their creativity. One of the basic principles of the book is that, because we are created, we are meant to create; it is a spiritual truth that "creativity is the natural order of life." I plunged into the recommended twelve-week course of reading and doing the recommended exercises at the end of each chapter, a week at a time. It required my rechecking the book four sequential times in three-week intervals to complete. Once I started, I was committed.

Words jumped off the page: "Our creative dreams and yearnings come from a divine source." Also, the book's suggested list of Creative

Affirmations included "My dreams come from God, and God has the power to accomplish them." This was counter to the ideology the church had planted in my mind at an impressionable age: that our wills always ran counter to God's will, and that our individual goals and dreams had to be sacrificed to remain in a right relationship with God.

One of the first exercises at the end of week one, "Recovering a Sense of Safety," was entitled Time Travel. It asked readers to identify "three old enemies" of their "creative self-worth." "Your historic monsters are the building blocks of your core negative beliefs." I wrote to the side of (1):

<u>Church</u>—when joined very conservative church—everything given up—no dance, gave up piano—

I loved to dance. Everything was meant to be sacrificed (though I loved singing in youth choir)

No living in the world as "part of the world"—separated from the secular.

Music in the church was all by ear—you had to have a gift for it—or so I thought.

My training was classical—so I didn't use my talent, because written music was not utilized

But encouraged my friend, who I traveled to Dallas with weekly for her private lesson.

Singing solos in church was also a "gift"—had to be humble, all for God— had to be "right with God."

I liked Drama in school—left it after Freshman year for Art the following year—

Can't remember why—unless wasn't cool to hang around geeky "weird drama kids"—

Or also no future in drama for me—Conflict of who I was in the church— limited goals or vision—everything through the church.

That same exercise suggested that "you might find it cathartic to draw a sketch of your old monster . . . Cartoon trashing your monster, or at least draw a nice red X through it."

<u>Cartoon image</u>—would be a skinny, homely girl in a <u>long skirt.</u>

Dress modest—<u>be humble</u>—no self-glorification. Do not draw attention to yourself. No self-pride—evil No self-promotion

**

Thirty years later, grieving over my mother in the form of self-worthlessness and failure, I hastily sketched in blue ink a miniature replica of my former self, the likes of which would never have attracted the eyes of a Todd Rundgren. I was still purging the church's influence over my thinking, and it was as if the voice of my mother was calling out to me . . . "Remember who you are."

The journey continued. I finished the book and plowed through it a second time at the author's suggestion. What followed were my heady attempts at giving myself a creative voice. My first attempt was poetry, which led to prose. I eventually found myself on the community stage. The people as well as shared experiences were as important as the opening of my mind into a world that I had been taught was dangerous.

It was freeing to be able to drive around in a minivan with a napping five-year-old while rock and roll from my past blasted throughout the interior, or—even better—when all three kids began to request their favorite songs on the way to school or soccer practice. The behavior was without condemnation, if I excluded the bewilderment of my husband. And damnation be damned if the guitars got a little loud, or if the lyrics referenced rebellion, sex, or just plain snarky takes on the establishment.

> *Save all your money, go confess on Sunday, Sweet Boy*
> *And you get your copy of Honey*
> *And back on the street by Monday*
> *. . . You don't have to camp around*
> **"You Don't Have to Camp Around," Todd Rundgren, 1973**

What's a *Honey*? Popular in the 1960s and '70s, it was a United Kingdom fashion tabloid—for progressive tastes—featuring the cover tagline, "Young, gay and get-ahead." I could even sing along once I mastered the words in time to the rhythm. To think I had missed out on prog-rock in my youth, because I was afraid of hell, and how ironic it was that it had taken the death of my mother for me to be able to listen to a song about a gay guy without freaking out. Playing Todd's CDs was just the beginning; I had friendships to make in the not-too-distant future that would challenge the nonsense I had been taught by providing real relational moments.

Chapter 22

Julia Cameron says, "Name your dream; write it down. In a perfect world, if you could go back and do over, what would you be; what could you be? Make an action plan to work toward your goal: five-year plan, a year from now, next month, next week, today—do something." *Okay. I want to participate in the arts. I want to be an actress, a published writer, a poet. Write and submit; try out for a part in the local theatre (even though they're really after my husband for the lead in their next show).*

And so, I did. Our local community theatre held auditions for *Little Shop of Horrors* in fall 2008. Mom had died the previous year and in the same month the show would open. Though I was in a better place after a bumpy year, restlessness had receded only slightly. I went along with my husband, who was wanted by the director for the part of Seymour. The stage musical, composed and written by Alan Menken and Howard Ashman, respectively, is especially popular with community theatres and high school drama departments because of its short list of characters. However, our local director wanted to utilize a larger portion of the community and expanded the cast list to include six roles representing the usual street urchin trio (patterned after a 1960s Motown group) that sets the scene and provides musical and dance commentary throughout the show. We were all white instead of the expected racial prototype, and older too, due in part to the demographic of community participation in local theatre. My character's take had a seasoned outlook on life due to my being older than the rest of the chorus. I named her Lois.

Returning to the stage was intimidating at first, particularly nailing down music sung to choreographed numbers (*Which foot goes where? What are my arms supposed to be doing? I'm expected to harmonize at the same time?*), but long hours of practice and newfound camaraderie among stage-loving amateurs helped smooth out the nerves and boosted my lack of confidence. In fact, the raunchier it got, the more fun: dirty dancing in the dressing rooms, rocking the outfits, or the off-color humor that permeated the musical. Certain people—because of previous stage experience, natural talent, or an inner sense of fun—captured this playful adult mood more than others. It was hard not to gravitate toward one individual, particularly when he stood 6'4". Sporting long khaki shorts after recent weight loss, he could be heard before he entered a room. His larger-than-life laugh identified him wherever he went.

He was simply introduced as our "music director," but I had visions of sitting down with this seasoned church organist and writing a play titled *BogotaVille*, based on the life and observations of a towering gay funeral director in a small town. Absorbing the magnitude of him was as equally entertaining as my initial chance to perform on the stage on which he had grown up. I was struck by his amazing musical talent, his sense of humor injected into every rehearsal (whether it was good or "a bitch" as he referred to them), and, above all, his flexibility due to the aforementioned. His unabashed commentary on all things quickly let me know he was younger but was greatly influenced by the arts and music of my youth. We soon forged a friendship that felt strangely familiar rather than alarming, considering his over-the-top personality. He was a catalyst: an agent that provoked a speedy significant change.

One night during a rehearsal break, my husband made an inoffensive but casual remark regarding life choices and consequences by certain groups, to which my large friend immediately responded. I now can recognize his usual reflexive habit of addressing even serious topics with humor; back then I couldn't. His face became animated with the arching of his eyebrows and targeting beady eyes as he interjected into every phrase that damn laugh. "It's no choice, Cliff. EH HAAGHHAA EH HAAGHHA! It isn't a choice. EH HAAGHHAA EH HAAGHHA!" Thirty-six years of encrusted scales fell from my eyes, shot out my ears, and landed on the floor of the theatre with a resounding clank. *People were who they were.*

With those words he managed to shake off a hell-damning ideology that had ensnared me from a time before I was even able to comprehend *what* I was even supposed to be warring against. Because it happened in the context of relationship, *it* no longer felt contagious. This worry over the business of *being evil by association* ceased. My husband's epiphany followed a couple of years later during a *poetry festival* he was dragged along to attend.

* * *

The 2 A.M. whistle of the long train stretches out the thread between days, pins it in a crack between its teeth and pulls so the people in white beds by the flour mill become the wheat unground in the sacks…
Fuel, Naomi Shihab Nye

Sometime in the middle of her first-grade year, my daughter came home from school, announcing I was to attend a book event for students and their parents. A local author from San Antonio would be coming to Helotes Elementary to share some readings from her books. My daughter issued the invitation so emphatically that it was assumed I would drop my busy schedule and run up to the school after dinner. I reluctantly complied, with her in tow.

The author was an internationally known poet, Naomi Shihab Nye, with whom I was unfamiliar. She read from her children's book *Lullaby Raft* and other selections of poetry before personally signing some of her books for purchase. Prior to her readings, she emphasized how poetry was a gift we should give ourselves every day. She told the story of once meeting a man who had been raised on an Oklahoma farm. He told her while growing up he had awakened every morning for school to the sound of his father reading poetry sitting in a chair next to his bed. No need for an alarm clock. Having been raised in North Texas (with its superiority complex regarding neighbors across the Red River), I thought, "Hell, if a farmer in Oklahoma, of all places, can enjoy reading poetry, so can I." But it took a while, years. Even though I purchased a few of Nye's books and one from a secondhand shop in town a week or so later, poetry lay dormant—until the death of my mother.

Poetry began in earnest while plowing through the weekly exercises designated at the end of each chapter in *The Artist's Way*—not good poetry but poetry *attempted,* nevertheless. Summoned either by courage from re-birthed creativity or by stupidity, I naively wrote Naomi via her publishing agent after an online search one night. I reminded her of our first meeting some nine years earlier and had the unmitigated gall to inquire "how to go about having one's poetry published?" The kicker was . . . she answered. She penned her response along the top and margins of my own letter, apologetically on her way to Morocco! She just happened to mention a gathering of poets she annually attended that took place every spring in the quaint Texas town of Round Top. Well, that was good enough for me. It must be a sign or something.

But the iris I moved from your house now hold in the dusty dry fists of
their roots green knives and forks as if waiting for dinner,
as if spring were a feast. I thank you for that.

> *Were it not for the way you taught me to look at the world,*
> *to see the life at play in everything,*
> *I would have to be lonely forever.*
> **Lights on a Ground of Darkness,** Ted Kooser

* * *

Spring 2010, I was surrounded by poetic greats such as Ted Kooser, two-time U.S. poet laureate, the late Brigit Pegeen Kelly, and Harryette Mullen; however, I was in search of Naomi. I wanted to thank her for answering my letter and let her know I had arrived for Poetry at Round Top. Egad! My enthusiasm and lack of tact knew no bounds during those days of carving out a creative niche. Thankfully, because of the heartfelt poet she is, she did remember corresponding with me after our initial hellos.

The marriage of written poetry and spoken performance was beyond all my expectations, when, of course, it was being executed at the festival by some of poetry's finest. I attended all the featured readings, panel discussions, and even an optional workshop, while my husband set out in his kayak for local fishing. We dined in the evenings in the basement of the fabulous historically preserved Menke House, followed by readings from the featured headliners in the opulent artisan-carved Festival Concert Hall, before rounding out the evenings with drinks and more readings in the basement of the Edythe Bates Old Chapel—all on the lush grounds of the Festival Institute just outside of Round Top, population 90 in the 2010 census. Besides the standing ovation for Ted Kooser atop the amber-lit stage in the majestic surrounding of the great performance hall, my most memorable moment happened after an open mic session on Saturday afternoon. Atop the same stage I nervously read a poem of mine entitled "The Trumpet Flower." Following the end of the open mic participants' reading, Naomi purposefully came up to me, reached for my arm, and pointedly but softly said, "Your poem moved me."

Aside from all the poetry and conversations, the friendships made lasted far longer than the lingering memory of exquisite verse. I stood on a pebbled drive and shared a three-way conversation with Ted Kooser and Harryette Mullins about their craft as I would have with a neighbor out by the mailbox. I would most likely never run into them again, but I would encounter others. As I repeatedly returned in the month of April for the festival, familiar faces eventually attached to their names would appear for joyful reunions with increasing poignancy, because some would all together cease coming for various reasons. Over the years, surprise marriages, publishing accomplishments, new appointments, diagnoses, and even death marked our encounters. All were shared, contributing to the lively conversations usually wrought with laughter that echoed throughout the Menke House during dinner.

Two women owners of a successful bookstore in Austin, Texas, are expected pillars at the spring gathering and lend to its success. They bring books in bulk of the featured poets along with a plethora of poetry chapbooks and hardcovers from other poets and display them for purchase inside the concert hall's entrance. One Saturday evening during a festival weekend, they were seated at our table along with a Methodist pastor and his wife. By the time I tuned into the conversation, the topic of homosexuality was in full swing as I caught the tail end of the pastor's take on the subject. He didn't consider the topic disconcerting or cause for condemnation because Jesus never remarked on the issue. And then my husband turned to one of the gay women sitting next to him and made a profound statement that changed everything. "Well, Paul says . . ." to which the woman immediately responded in earnest consternation, "Who's Paul?"

Now, I had already put to rest biblical passages declaring "man lying with mankind as he lieth with a woman" *an abomination*, when other Hebrew traditions associated with this term included Old Testament "touching or eating anything unclean," "winged insects with four feet," "differing weights and measures," "animal sacrifices with a single blemish," and "scoffers," to name a few. The woman's response took Cliff totally by surprise. Later that night, he relayed to me how irrelevant his point must have sounded to someone who was totally unfamiliar with one of the writers in a text he had been familiar with since a child, having been raised in that tradition. By late afternoon the following day, he had reached his own conclusion during uninterrupted, deep contemplation while fishing on the lake: *"People are just who they are."*

Chapter 23

My brother and his wife annually host a barbecue potluck, featuring his tender smoked beef brisket and a longtime friend's homemade ice cream the Saturday of Memorial Day weekend. It takes place on the same spot of land once owned by our uncle. Such was the setting where I reunited with my cousin Diana, years after having briefly spoken with her at her father's graveside service in 2010. She decided to drive up from South Texas to reconnect with family and friends she hadn't seen since moving back to Texas.

This visitation occurred before the beginning of summer 2014. I had already signed up with Battleground Texas to help get the vote out for Wendy Davis, Democrat candidate running for governor of Texas, in the upcoming fall election. I had become increasingly aware of the tactics of Greg Abbott, acting attorney general under the weary, long tenure of Governor Rick Perry. When Greg Abbott began carving away at the Voting Rights Act of 1964 by enacting Texas' voter ID law in 2011, I decided to get off the couch and do something. I had long been off the fence regarding constitutional interpretations and discriminations surrounding social issues; undermining the Civil Rights Movement's long-fought battle for voter equality galled me to the root.

Abbott was born two years before me; surely, he witnessed the same news headlines that were imprinted in my memory, or perhaps they had affected him differently. I could go back to the spot in the road where I first heard the news that Martin Luther King Jr. had been shot. The interrupted radio broadcast announcing his death occurred many springs past, on our way home from visiting my grandparents. From the backseat I watched my father turn to my mother and express fear over sure retribution from the black community: "They won't be able to control them now. No telling what will take place." I was eight years old.

***

It was refreshingly like old times, visiting with my cousin little over a mile from where our old playhouses once stood. We seemed to take up from where we had left off—no awkwardness or regrets. My ease probably had more to do with being freed from an unnecessary propagated stance and acknowledging, without fear, the problems others were experiencing, locally and abroad. She desired reconnection. "Yeah, I told myself I'd probably be the only Democrat here, but I don't care; I wanted to see everybody," she stated. "I decided I would be like Daddy always said, 'Just be kind and respectful.' But not everybody acts like that these days." "Well, I can assure you, you're not the only one who thinks differently. You're not alone," I said.

After lunch, we had separated from the rest of the group and were hanging out along my brother's fence line in conversation. I brought up the recent progressive changes regarding gay marital rights following the Supreme Court's ruling on the Defense of Marriage Act in 2013.

"Can you believe some of the changes taking place?" I asked, remembering the civil union with her longtime partner that had occurred in California years previously.

"Well, the military is the reason for recent progress," she observed. "Overturning 'Don't Ask, Don't Tell' has led the way; once we got past that, things have started to move forward."

We continued our remembrances of days past with our grandparents while relating current happenings of shared family. Her sister Karen was in Tucson, Arizona, rehabilitating from a terrible accident. A previously convicted intoxicated driver had t-boned her motor scooter, crushing her left leg and hip, resulting in amputation of both after two years. Things hadn't seemed to have changed much between the two; communication had been sparse. Otherwise, the day was bright, and talk continued as if we had bridged the gap of missing years, conversing on the same rock drive where we had gathered after her graduation thirty-six years earlier. I was to think on these things just a few months down the road.

I spent summer 2014 entrenched within Battleground Texas, registering voters, hosting phone banks, and canvassing neighborhoods in Northeast Texas. Every Saturday morning for six months I printed out assigned eligible voters and left on my bicycle with water, pen, and campaign brochures—topped off with a straw cowboy hat that shielded me from the blistering heat that didn't let up until October. During one of those long hot Saturdays, I stood on the porch of a mauve and pinkish-tan home in the middle of a row of modest houses, listening to the strummed strings of a guitar from inside. The man of the house answered the door knock after laying aside his instrument.

He was friendly, and we began to talk about the upcoming election after I introduced myself as a neighbor in his community representing the Democrat Party's candidate in the governor's race. The conversation remained polite but shifted rather quickly to his religious views on certain social issues. He was an avid fan of John Hagee (courtesy of cable TV), a fire-and-brimstone evangelical pastor of a non-denominational church in San Antonio, Texas. Having once lived just down the road from the large religious complex, I nodded, "Yeah, I know him." He continued to expound on his admiration of the man and his *true* biblical preaching and vowed, if he lived closer, he would surely attend Hagee's church. Soon enough the man's biblical views turned to discussing homosexuality and his concern for "helping those people." The right teaching from the Bible could "convert these people from their ways," a viewpoint he approached with all sincerity, as noted by the look on his face.

Within the shade of his porch I gently began to tell stories of growing up with my two cousins. It was the first time I had ever relayed to anybody a viewpoint on homosexuality based on my real-life relations. It had suddenly become crystal clear and timely relevant. I calmly retold our playhouse rules and role assignments and how these same roles had been entrenched within my two cousins from their early years. We were cousins parented by two brothers who shared the same set of parents and upbringing. To think of us as anything different would have never crossed our minds. "She was the dad, and I was the mother, always, period." He looked upon me with momentary interest and then proceeded talking ad nauseam. My captivity ended after he finally closed the door. I shook my head at the time I had lost while listening to his *testimony*. Our encounter would surely be something worth sharing with his Sunday School class the following morning.

The November 2014 election in Texas did not go as I had hoped. In fact, I was downright devastated at the opportunity Texas missed. Within this shadow of election results, I received a call from my Battleground field organizer, asking me to come to Fayetteville, Arkansas. "You're a proponent for civil rights, right? Well, we need you to block-walk this weekend for a very important cause." So, I set out for Arkansas late on a Friday afternoon with the promise of free lodging with a local family, a paper map, outdated cell phone, and address of a restaurant where several organizers would be dining. With some trepidation I watched the sun setting while beginning my trek up through the Talimena Pass, a two-lane road in the Winding Stair

Mountains spanning Eastern Oklahoma to Western Arkansas. A heavy rain ensued, worsening the total eclipse of light in the surrounding Ouachita National Forest. I gratefully followed the soft red glow of a semi-trailer's taillights until I reached the interstate, well into Northern Arkansas.

Dinner was a delightful reunion with some Battleground organizers who were recapping and buffering the devastating election results with humor and alcohol. I was then given my charge and a bit of background history.

On August 19, the city council of Fayetteville had adopted Civil Rights Administration Ordinance 119 by a six-to-two vote. The ordinance extended the protected rights guaranteed to citizens in the Arkansas 1964 Civil Rights Acts to include categories of gender ID and gender preferences, joining over 185 major cities and counties nationwide with similar protections. It also created a municipal civil rights administrator position to *investigate* discrimination complaints. Led by evangelical Republicans outside of Fayetteville, opposition group Repeal 119 was formed and collected enough signatures to force a special election that would cost the taxpayers $40,000. An organization, Family Council, spent large sums of money toward the repeal. Jim Bob and Michelle Duggar, of the *19 Kids and Counting* TLC network reality series, donated $10,000. Michelle recorded an automated telephone message for ominous robo calls that centered on "safety" for women and children in public restrooms while encouraging votes against the equal rights ordinance for LGBT citizens.

"Hello, this is Michelle Duggar. I'm calling to inform you of some shocking news that would affect the safety of Northwest Arkansas women and children. The Fayetteville city council is voting on an ordinance this Tuesday night that would allow men—yes, I said men— to use women's and girls' restrooms, locker rooms, showers, sleeping areas and other areas that are designated for females only. I don't believe the citizens of Fayetteville would want males with past child predator convictions that claim they are female to have a legal right to enter private areas that are reserved for women and girls. I doubt that Fayetteville parents would stand for a law that would endanger their daughters or allow them to be traumatized by a man joining them in their private space. We should never place the preference of an adult over the safety and innocence of a child. Parents, who do you want undressing next to your daughter at the public swimming pool's private changing area? I still believe that we are a society that puts women and children first. Women, young ladies and little girls deserve to use the restroom or any other facility in peace and safety...."

* * *

After meeting and receiving instructions from the group Keep Fayetteville Fair—in support of Fayetteville's Civil Rights Ordinance—I set off to canvass my designated neighborhood voters. I was armed with the knowledge that Arkansas state laws already prohibited people from attempting to enter the wrong bathroom for any unlawful purpose (in case the words of a fecund woman from Tontitown, Arkansas, needed clarification). I knocked on specified doors and encouraged voters to check "Against Repeal" in the slated election, walking amidst Vote Against Repeal signs and vivid purple Vote For Appeal signs posted throughout the town. And yes, I saw confusion register on more than a few faces regarding the two opposing political slogans. I left for home late Sunday afternoon after meeting some great people, but I felt the same skepticism I had prior to the Texas mid-term election. The ordinance was repealed by a margin of 51.6% to 48.3% (7,523 votes to 7,040).

That Sunday morning prior to block-walking, I spoke with an organizer from one of the two groups involved, Keep Fayetteville Fair or Human Rights Campaign in Arkansas, about the religious right's involvement. "I don't think people in general or those within mainstream protestant churches have any idea how bizarre or extreme this can get," I told him. "I was young when I peeled away from my formal protestant teaching and spent six years in a very fundamentalist church that makes all this fear of 'bathroom talk' pale in comparison to the hell-condemning rhetoric I heard during my formative years. Homosexuality was considered an evil spirit. It was the spirit of the world that was prophesied in the book of Revelation's *last days*. It would bring judgment upon *all* associated. If you were sympathetic to or associated with gays, you were 'sympathetic to the devil,' and you were exposing yourself and your family to an evil spirit that would take over and dwell in you." The young man looked at me with widened eyes as if I had let him in on a secret he had never heard.

* * *

> Act 137 was approved by Arkansas state legislature in February 2015 to prevent any local anti-discrimination law that went beyond the state's laws against discrimination. The Uniform Civil Rights Protection Ordinance 5781, a measure seeking to prohibit discrimination based on sexual orientation or gender identity, was approved by Fayetteville voters of Washington County on September 8, 2015, 52.79% to 47.21% (7,698 votes to 6,884). It provided an exemption for "churches, religious schools and daycare facilities, and religious organizations of any kind." On February 23, 2017, the Arkansas Supreme Court overturned Ordinance 5781, ruling that it violated Act 137.
>
> As activists have turned to local ballot measures to push agendas such as bans on genetically modified organisms (GMOs), higher minimum wages, LGBT anti-

discrimination ordinances, marijuana legalization, and anti-fracking restrictions, advocates of opposing agendas have teamed with some who think that power over certain issues should belong exclusively to state governments to diminish the authority of local government entities. In some states, opposition to local ballot measures concerning contentious issues has been shown by officials at the state level, and conflict between the authority of local government entities and state governments has become an important narrative in U.S. politics.

Ballotpedia: City of Fayetteville LGBT "Uniform Civil Rights Protection Ordinance," Ordinance 5781 (September 2015)

Chapter 24

So, now I was an activist. I was suddenly defending the rights of individuals with whom the church had aggressively instructed me to avoid, even by disassociation. Because of its teachings and fear-mongering prayer sessions behind closed doors in the designated prayer room, I had subsequently become uncomfortable in situational associations with those whose "lifestyle choices" were tattooed an *abomination*. Though my day-to-day interactions, whether social or professional, bade me treat people cordially, a red flag immediately waved at the first hint of a person's having an alternative sexual view or orientation. The fact I had not stepped inside the church I left in 1978, nor had intention of ever darkening its doors after my life-altering depression in 1997, did little to abate the unease I felt discussing homosexuality. The very word brought angst.

I once left a favorite male stylist who had done makeup and hair for my wedding after he exclaimed, "Who's that?" while pointing with exaggerated interest to one of my husband's groomsmen in our wedding album. I sat as far away as possible and avoided contact with a lesbian couple in our Methodist church choir. I felt sorry for the small, beautiful Vietnamese girl they adopted. I kept polite distance during medical school and residency from those I suspected were homosexual, even though I might have liked or respected them professionally. And I vocalized my consternation when my cousin's partner underwent in-vitro fertilization, so they could parent a child together. "What is Diana thinking? If they split, she will not have any right to the child," I had fumed. A homophobic strand had indeed been woven within the spiritual thread of my being. Shortly after the death of my mom, it began to silently unravel.

On June 26, 2015, I stopped in the middle of my bike ride to answer a call from my daughter. She was excitedly announcing the Supreme Court's ruling on same-sex marriage. Standing to the side of the road astride my bike, I immediately started scrolling through Facebook to read the national news and varied reactions. One post stood out. A close friend, who, two years before, had lost his partner wrote something to the effect that he had planned to watch the Court's announcement with distant interest, because it would have little impact on his current grief. When the news broke, he discovered instead that he burst into unprovoked tears. I pedaled home excitedly under a sunlit sky to peruse more news reports of the historic day.

Sitting on the back patio with my family, I began to read via social media all the news leading to the historic change and noted with interest some preparations in our own small conservative community of Paris, Texas, the county seat of Lamar County. Russ Towers, county clerk, had issued a statement to the local paper the previous day, stating he would issue marriage licenses as soon as the district attorney said he could if the Supreme Court ruled in favor of same-sex marriage. I had gone to Russ as a resource when I was busy registering voters for the 2014 mid-term election, and we had participated together in addressing students at our local junior college at the request of one of its instructors about the importance of voting. I had been told Russ was gay; based on our professional dealings, I wasn't sure he was openly gay.

On Facebook, my good friend, photographer Ginger Cook, wrote: "I must say I am a little overwhelmed at the moment. You should have seen me running over to the Lamar County Courthouse from my studio with my camera in hand just after 1 p.m. Dacey and Brittany allowed me to photograph them just after receiving their marriage license. They are the first gay couple to be married in Lamar County, Texas. It was an honor to photograph such a historic moment. It was a memorable day for County Clerk Russ Towers and his staff as well."

Soon after, Russ posted: "I just issued my first marriage license to a same sex couple!!" Like millions of others, he had pasted a rainbow flag over his Facebook profile picture to *celebrate pride*, using a photo-editing tool Facebook had launched that Friday. Upon seeing his profile page, I, like my friend, suddenly shed unexpected tears. I turned to my husband, enjoying our celebratory margaritas: "Do you realize how these people have been living? Do we have any idea what this means to them?"

Russ would, in fact, go on to issue three marriage licenses to same-sex couples on the first day. Earlier that same day he had posted: "Growing up as a gay man, I never thought I would see the day that same sex couples would be able to publicly proclaim their love for each other through marriage that will hopefully soon be recognized by Federal and all State Governments. The really exciting part is that, as a County clerk, I will be able to take part in history by issuing marriage licenses to same sex couples. I believe that I was chosen for this job for this reason!"

Reveling in my own celebratory freedom from bias in the summer of 2015 momentarily sheltered me from the darkening clouds that were beginning to form. I would soon learn that the punitive homophobic views espoused by the religious cult of my adolescence had been welded into a powerful political tool embraced by many in mainstream religious America.

Chapter 25

I wonder what my trajectory toward views on homosexuality and gender identification would have been if my twelve-year-old self had not accepted that invitation from a neighborhood friend to attend Sunday night church services. I wonder if I would have regarded my cousins and their adult evolvement as natural, if I had not gone back to answer the church's altar call, if the momentum hadn't carried me away from my own family's approach toward religious instruction. I wonder if swallowing beliefs from an intensely charismatic, cult-like church community precluded me from growing up unbiased regarding views on sexual relations that would have eventually presented themselves for my consideration. I wonder if I would have come around sooner.

Perhaps I would have been influenced by the southern culture around me, the primarily protestant, conservative views of others regarding sexuality that differed from mainstream, "somewhere out there on the East or West coast." Perhaps I would have mirrored the views of my family regarding our *own homosexuals* as a slightly embarrassing topic, something we talked about in secret, even something we snickered over or winked at one another during conversation regarding their indiscretion. Perhaps I would have naturally come to an understanding as I matured and became comfortable with my own sexuality. Perhaps my worldview would have evolved on pace with the increasingly accepting culture when it became evident that many acquaintances—even friends and family—were gay. Perhaps I would have been as open-minded as my cousin on Mother's side of the family. Linda never felt a sense of unease when she saw images of intimacy between two same-sex individuals. She saw it as two people in love: "Wasn't that nice."

Surely, I would not have viewed homosexuality as an evil spirit that would infect me and my family simply by associating with individuals who were homosexual. I don't think I ever would have regarded it as a plague: a "spirit of the age" that would bring God's wrath upon the whole earth, resulting in its final judgment, not to mention the preceding natural disasters as its direct consequence. I hope I would have faced my developing awareness with more compassion, acceptance, and less fear.

***

But these things do not cloud my memory of a time when shortening days heralded an approaching winter holiday while my cousins and I prepared a home together in the chicken brooder shed. Before supper we were busy in our own kitchen, preparing our meal with collected utensils on child-sized tin plates imprinted with images of Mary's Little Lamb. Our voices in fervent play fall gently on my ears, from a place where all was right and limitless.

"Okay, let's play 'House.' Pretend this is our kitchen and living room. That is our bedroom. Let's pretend I'm the mother. Dini, you're the father. Let's pretend it's a hard, cold winter, and Father is coming in from the fields, and I'm fixin' dinner. Karen, you can be the son, and you're gathering the wood. And then let's pretend . . . ."

About the Author

Sherry Scott is a writer and medical doctor who has practiced palliative/hospice care for children. She is the author of *The Year My Mother Died*, 2011, and *The People of Nineteenth Street*, 2018. She serves as vice president of the Gendercide Awareness Project in Dallas, Texas, and lives in Paris, Texas, with her family.

Note from the Author

Word-of-mouth is crucial for any author to succeed. If you enjoyed *Playhouses*, please leave a review online—anywhere you are able—even if it's just a sentence or two. It would make all the difference and would be very much appreciated.

Thanks!
Sherry Scott

We hope you enjoyed reading this title from:

www.blackrosewriting.com

Subscribe to our mailing list – *The Rosevine* – and receive **FREE** books, daily deals, and stay current with news about upcoming releases and our hottest authors.
Scan the QR code below to sign up.

Already a subscriber? Please accept a sincere thank you for being a fan of Black Rose Writing authors.

View other Black Rose Writing titles at www.blackrosewriting.com/books and use promo code **PRINT** to receive a **20% discount** when purchasing.

www.ingramcontent.com/pod-product-compliance
Lightning Source LLC
Chambersburg PA
CBHW071902070526
44583CB00016B/1809